The Dialectic of Selfhood
in Montaigne

FREDERICK RIDER

The Dialectic of Selfhood
in Montaigne

Stanford University Press

Stanford, California

1973

Stanford University Press
Stanford, California
© 1973 by the Board of Trustees of the
Leland Stanford Junior University
Printed in the United States of America
ISBN 0-8047-0830-4
LC 72-91679

Preface

Encountering Montaigne has been for me a process of personal development. For introducing him to me, and for guiding and encouraging me through each stage in the ensuing relationship, Harry Berger, Jr., has my gratitude. His contributions to this essay have become indistinguishable from my own. To those who helped along the way, sometimes more than they knew—especially Norman O. Brown, Bernd Jager, Albert Hofstadter, and George Boas—I also extend my thanks. C. L. Barber, John Hummel, and Thomas A. Vogler read earlier versions of the manuscript and helped to repair some of its deficiencies. I am particularly grateful for their thoughtful criticism, for the understanding and expeditious secretarial aid of Carolyn Brown, and for the financial support of the Danforth Foundation, which relieved me of teaching duties while I was writing.

F.J.R.

Contents

Note on the Translations

The translations of Montaigne used in this study are based on three sources. The most important of these is the Pléiade edition of the *Oeuvres complètes*, edited by Thibaudet and Rat; page references to this volume are preceded by the letters *OC*. The corresponding translations are from the Stanford edition of the *Complete Essays*, translated by Donald M. Frame; references to this edition are preceded by the letter *S*. It has frequently been necessary for me to cite the earliest version of the *Essais*, published in 1580 and reproduced in the edition of Dezeimeris and Barckhausen; my references then begin with the letters *DB*.

In translating the *DB* text, I have followed Frame as closely as possible, deviating only where the French wording differs from that of *OC*. However, for the convenience of the reader who may not have access to the *DB* edition, I have cited parallel passages in *OC* and in *S* whenever possible, although they frequently differ from the earlier version in minor ways.

Complete information on the various editions I have used will be found under Montaigne in the Bibliography, pp. 105–7.

Professor Frame's translations are used with the kind permission of Stanford University Press.

*The Dialectic of Selfhood
in Montaigne*

Introduction

The theme of this book is human development, as seen in one of its more important and particular manifestations. My subject will be six essays by Michel de Montaigne, each examined in its successive revisions over a period of twelve to twenty years. I shall try to understand each essay as a response to circumstances in Montaigne's life, and further, to understand his personal development in terms of the various responses that he formulates in the essays.

Developmental approaches to the essays of Montaigne are hardly new, and were undertaken with considerable success by such critics as Pierre Villey and Fortunat Strowski in the early years of this century. In reaction to Villey's overemphasis on the literary sources of Montaigne's work, F. J. B. Jansen wrote on the psychological and biographical foundations of the essays (1935); and two decades later, Donald M. Frame attempted to synthesize the two views and to deepen their insights, feeling that "a more organic theory would show the unfolding of Montaigne's thought as a progressive liberation from apprehension and tutelage." In Frame's words will be found the germ of my own interpretation; but I shall attempt to examine more closely the sources of human apprehension, the mechanisms of tutelage, the process by which a person "liberates" himself, and the limitations inherent in the particular form of progress made by Montaigne. In other words, I shall attempt to make explicit some of the psychological assumptions that are merely implicit in other interpretations of his development.[1]

Such an effort requires that Montaigne's psychological discoveries be continually compared with our own conceptions of human nature, that his observations and our theories correct and enrich one another. As the reader will see, I have borrowed many notions from twentieth-century thinkers with no justification beyond the fact that they seem to illuminate Montaigne's text without reducing him to a case history. In general, these are of three sorts.

First, there is my overall view of human development as a dialectic in which biological process and social process become thesis and antithesis, with ego process as a synthesizer. Individuation is seen as a series of crises in which the various components of a personality are either integrated by the ego or lapse into some form of disintegration. In this approach I follow the well-known works of Erik H. Erikson. I also embrace Erikson's holistic bias—the conviction that the individual, whom we may analyze from biological, social, or egological perspectives, is in fact an indivisible unity.[2] (Montaigne would have agreed: "Il est plustost à croire qu'il ne s'engendre rien en un corps que par la conspiration et communication de toutes les parties."[3])

[1] See Villey, *Les Sources et l'évolution des essais de Montaigne.* Strowski, *Montaigne: Sa vie publique et privée.* Jansen, *Sources vives de la penseé de Montaigne.* Frame, *Montaigne's Discovery of Man,* p. 7.

[2] Erikson, *Childhood and Society, Young Man Luther, Insight and Responsibility,* and *Identity: Youth and Crisis.* I have found Merleau-Ponty's *Structure of Behavior* a valuable philosophical supplement to Erikson's social-scientific approach to holism.

[3] *OC,* p. 759. (For complete information on the various editions of Mon-

Second, to explain the success or failure of the ego in its integrative task, I have borrowed a group of ideas from existialist philosophy. These center on Kierkegaard's intuition that anxiety is a response to freedom. The relations between anxiety, fear, freedom, and self-actualization, dealt with at length by Heidegger, have been stated with great clarity on the psychological plane by Kurt Goldstein. I have also tended to assimilate the psychoanalytic notions of ambivalence, defense, and repression to Sartre's concept of bad faith, the generalized motive for which is a flight from freedom and anxiety. The alternative to this flight, manifested in successful self-actualization, I have termed "courage," as Paul Tillich does.[4]

Third, I have used a structural conception that divides the self into object and process. Although I have reworked this idea considerably in order to apply it to Montaigne, it derives from such diverse writers as George H. Mead, Erikson, and Sartre.[5] The term "ego" I use to denote the self as process, as agent, or as subject; its functions are roughly those Mead assigns to the "I." The term "Self" (which I shall capitalize to reduce confusion) denotes the self as object, roughly equivalent to Mead's "me." The essential point to remark here is that the ego cannot observe itself, but can only construct a Self to observe. I use "self," when not capitalized, to mean an entity comprehending both the Self and the ego—i.e., to indicate reflexivity without differentiating subject and object.

---

taigne's works that I have used, see under Montaigne in the Bibliography, pp. 105–7.

[4] Kierkegaard, *The Concept of Dread.* Heidegger, *Being and Time.* Goldstein, *Human Nature in the Light of Psychopathology.* Sartre, *Being and Nothingness* and *Existential Psychoanalysis.* Tillich, *The Courage To Be.*

[5] Mead, *Mind, Self and Society.* Sartre, *The Transcendence of the Ego.* The reader should be warned that my usage of the terms "self," "Self," and "ego" is not precisely that of either Mead or Sartre. My terms have been chosen with reference to varied usage in American psychology, as summarized by Hall and Lindzey, pp. 515–23.

3

In Montaigne's case, I shall be studying an exteriorization of the Self in the form of a literary self-portrait—or, as I shall call it, Montaigne's self-image. The role of image-making in human development has been analyzed by Hans Jonas, and some of my conclusions will rest on his work. Certain other ideas on the relation between imagination, identification, and language have been suggested to me by the writings of Anthony Wilden and Jacques Lacan, though I confess I am still disoriented in their house of mirrors.[6]

Such are my sources in psychology. But my intentions are not exclusively psychological, for I am equally interested in demonstrating the coherence of individual essays as expressions of a continuing development, and in assessing their place in that transformation of consciousness that we call the Renaisssance. Six of the nine chapters following, therefore, are interpretations of Montaigne's texts, since it is in the concrete texts that literature, history, and psychology become indistinguishable.

[6] Jonas, *The Phenomenon of Life*; Sartre, *The Psychology of Imagination*, is also relevant to this problem. Lacan, "Le Stade du miroir comme formateur de la fonction du Je" and "The Function of Language in Psychoanalysis." Wilden, "Pars divers moyens on arrive à pareille fin."

1. The Need for Self-Distance

Ce qu'ils voulaient, ce qu'ils ont tenté—c'est la restauration de
l'unité mentale, le rêve de tous les hommes.
　　—LUCIEN FEBVRE, *Le Problème de l'incroyance au* XVI⁰ *siècle*

The extraordinary outpouring of self-interpretation that took
place at the beginning of the modern era—a movement in
which Montaigne was a leading but far from lonely figure—
implies that the men of that time recognized a new degree of
separation between the self and others, between self and self.
Interpretation and mediation are only required where there is
a chasm to be bridged.

It is a commonplace that every man of the Renaissance, in
particular every literate man, was intensely aware of differences, and often conflicts, in many aspects of life. The revival
of ancient literature presented him with a picture of a self-
sufficient and prestigious culture that had flourished in a time
other than his own. And the discovery of new continents revealed another side of his spatial world and presently existing
alternatives to his culture. Economic change, social mobility,
and plurality of roles were hardly new in the world, but the
Renaissance was a time when they were much in evidence, as
we shall see in Montaigne's case.

After the rise of centralized monarchies and the dissolu-
tion of a universal sense of Christendom, a man's national

allegiance assumed new importance, as did the characteristics distinguishing him from men of other nations. The elaboration and increasing rigidity of the Roman Church moved it ever farther from its spiritual foundations; practice and doctrine were often irreconcilable. From this conflict sprang the Protestant Reformation, disputing title to the very Kingdom of God. Men were not called upon simply to choose between orthodoxy and heresy: they had to make the much more difficult choice between authority and experience. The second dichotomy has many facets, and the shift from medieval to Renaissance consciousness was so complex a phenomenon that it defies analysis in terms of cause and effect. But it is evident that printed books were a principal source of man's awareness of difference, and also a potent means of response to it.

One characteristically human reaction to conflict is to step away from it and get an overall view, to "put it into perspective," to put *distance*, either physical or mental, between oneself and the objects that one must comprehend and control.[1] In any survey of Renaissance attitudes and behavior, three kinds of distance can be detected. The first, which puts distance between the self and the social world, might be called "individualism." The second, generally called "self-consciousness," divides the individual into subject and object, and one observes oneself across the distance between ego and Self. A third kind of distance appears in much of the art and literature of the period: the distance between the individual and an image of himself that he externalizes through the medium of written words or paint. This process, by which the self-image becomes an independent object visible both to oneself and to others, I will call "self-objectification."

Distance, in one or more of these aspects, is involved in all the familiar developments that characterize the Renaissance:

[1] See Jonas, Chapters VI–VII.

6

skepticism; the appeal to judgment, observation, and experience; the exploration of imaginary worlds; the distinction between public and private selves; and the gap between self and social role.[2] But rather than attempting to formulate general propositions about the functions of self-distance in Renaissance consciousness, I prefer to study its emergence in an individual life. Why was Montaigne impelled to objectify himself at a particular moment in history, and how did he accomplish it?

POLITICAL AND RELIGIOUS TENSIONS

Starting from the social periphery and moving toward the personal center, let us first observe that Michel Eyquem de Montaigne was born in 1533 at his family estate some thirty miles from the city of Bordeaux.[3] By virtue of his geographical origin he always considered himself a Gascon, although he never spoke the regional language. Gascony had been under English rule from 1154 to 1451, and its inhabitants may have felt some lingering identification with the English that retarded their absorption into the monarchy of France. There is little apparent trace in Montaigne's writings of this identification, but he shows a good deal of Gascon independence. He wants very much to be a Frenchman, and goes to great lengths to display his loyalty to the crown; but he is also proud of his country bluntness, and of a vocabulary that strikes his Parisian readers as quaint.

[2] The structural relations between these typically Renaissance attitudes are discussed by Harry Berger and H. M. Leicester in "An Approach to a Working Model of Period Consciousness." Goffman's "Role Distance" is also helpful here.

[3] The principal sources for my biographical account include, of course, the innumerable disclosures scattered throughout the *Essays*, Frame's *Montaigne: A Biography*, and the works of Strowski and Villey previously cited. The recent appearance of Roger Trinquet's authoritative work *La Jeunesse de Montaigne* has made it possible to correct many points that were previously in doubt or error.

Montaigne's ancestry was divided, his father coming from an old Bordeaux family of Catholic bourgeois, and his mother descending from Spanish merchants who may have been "new Christians" converted from Judaism during the preceding century. It is doubtful that Montaigne was aware of any Jewish heritage that he may have possessed, but he could scarcely remain unaware of another religious division that affected him. Southwestern France had been a center of religious as well as political revolt ever since the Albigensian Crusade had brought northern French Catholics into the area to crush the heretical Cathars in the early 1200's. And as recently as 1534 the *affaire des placards* had incited the wrath of Francis I against the new brand of heretics known as Huguenots, whose strength lay especially in the Southwest. Bordeaux was a Catholic town surrounded by refractory Protestant nobles. Coming as they did from the urban class, Montaigne's forebears were Catholic; but in his own generation at least two members of the family, his brother Thomas de Beauregard and his sister Jeanne de Lestonnac, turned to the Reform, and several of his schoolmasters were suspected of heresy. At the national, regional, and domestic levels, then, Protestantism was a momentous issue in his life.

PUBLIC AND PRIVATE WORLDS

The difference between the public and private worlds of Montaigne could hardly have been greater. In several essays (notably I: 26) he describes his extraordinary upbringing. His father, Pierre Eyquem de Montaigne, inspired by humanistic notions acquired on a campaign in Italy, determined to raise his "Micheau" in a manner then unknown among the French nobility. On the advice of experts, Pierre adopted the radical educational theories of Erasmus, which prescribed for the child a liberal regime and a thorough immersion in ancient languages from the age of two or three onward. Awakened with music each morning, corrected only with words, Michel was smiled upon and encouraged to be independent. He was given a tutor who spoke excellent Latin but no French and was addressed solely in Latin by parents and servants, absorbing ancient culture before he knew his own. Under this system he rapidly acquired an easy familiarity with letters and an intellectual approach to most of life's problems. Active mentally but idle physically, he was undisciplined in both respects.

Halfway through this experiment, he tells us, his father's nerve failed, and at six years of age Michel was uprooted from the gardens of the family estate to be shut up within the walls of the Collège de Guyenne in Bordeaux. This newly founded institution was liberal for its time, and our precocious Latinizer was given special treatment; even so, he must have found the college a depressing place. Boys of six and seven were required to study without recreation from early morning until late afternoon. Worse yet, they struggled to decipher elementary lines of a language in which he was already expert, while their intimate conversations were babbled in a vernacular that he was only beginning to understand.

Although there were some forty single holidays each year that Michel could spend with relatives in the city, only one vacation (ten days in September) was long enough for him to revisit the château. None of his fellow students could have shared his enthusiasm for Ovid and Terence, whose works he read on the sly. Indeed, most sons of the French nobility who attended a college, lacking his easy acquaintance with Latin, seem to have acquired a life-long hatred of things intellectual. Though exempted, on his father's orders, from the corporal punishment that was normally used to keep the students at their work, Michel must have keenly resented the pedantry and petty tyranny of collegiate life. It is certain that school taught him how to withdraw from society into the world of books—to reflect on everything, keep his opinions to himself, and seek pleasure in imagination.

9

The private world of his family home had a special primacy for Montaigne not only because it was so much pleasanter than the public world of the college, but also because it was the first world he knew, and because it was so soon abandoned. Everything that came afterward was not a part of that world; it was foreign to him, open to question and subject to adjustment. Very early he felt what it is to be *different*—standing outside his society, but thereby free to change himself and it.[4]

Although Montaigne's late adolescence is entirely undocumented, it is probable that he acquired an advanced general education in Paris, attending the courses of the *lecteurs royaux* and moving in fairly cosmopolitan circles.[5] In later life he was constantly shuttling between three places: the Château de Montaigne, where he wrote and lived with his close-knit family; Bordeaux, where he served in the Parlement and enjoyed the society of jurists, among whom were many who affected humanistic learning and several who were his relatives; and Paris, where he dealt with publishers and offered his services to the court. Indeed, when we view his life as a whole, our most constant image of him is on horseback. He sought opportunities to keep in motion between his various pleasures and responsibilities; and it was always on horseback, he says, that he had his best ideas.

Montaigne never seemed to doubt that the *raison d'être* of a gentleman is public service. For thirteen years as a counselor in the Bordeaux Parlement, for four years as mayor of Bordeaux, and almost to the end of his life as an adviser or secret negotiator for governors and kings, he accepted this as his duty. And although he sometimes bestirred himself only grudgingly in later life—the king had to press him, for in-

[4] Peter L. Berger and Thomas Luckmann have compared the process of "primary socialization" to the learning of one's native language: all languages subsequently learned can only be accretions to the first, lacking its power to structure our reality in a total and fundamental way. P. L. Berger and Luckmann, pp. 143–44.

[5] Trinquet, pp. 509–85.

stance, to accept the mayorality—as a young man he was not without ambition. Yet his obvious nostalgia for the ease of childhood, his enthusiasm for travel and private pastimes, and the mellowness of his final essays all testify to the fact that his supreme personal value was not virtue, valor, or responsibility, but happiness. And he was happiest in private, whether flirting with a lady, musing over a book, or engaging in spirited conversation.

One relationship of Montaigne's early life, however, firmly united his opposing tendencies toward self-actualization and comfort: his friendship with Etienne de la Boétie. During his late twenties, in fact, Montaigne found in La Boétie a mirror image so attractive that he almost lost sight of himself.[6] The essay "Of Friendship" describes this phenomenon in extended metaphors that I shall not attempt to reproduce or surpass. What interests me here is the fact that this friendship with a brilliant young humanist and magistrate provided Montaigne with both an intensely private bond and a model of what his public life should be. But La Boétie died suddenly, and some seventeen years passed before Montaigne found another means of connecting his public and private worlds.

PLURAL ROLES

Montaigne on horseback is symbolic of a man continually in movement not only between public and private domains but also between different social roles. If he acquired the habit of solitary reflection and began to think of it as the activity most characteristic of his identity, it may be because his public roles were so many and so varied. In Montaigne's life we can distinguish at least six principal roles.

It is evident from Montaigne's early education that his father hoped he would become a learned man—not a scholar in the professional sense, but a man so at home with the clas-

---

[6] On Montaigne's "loss of his self" in that of La Boétie, see the penetrating interpretation by Anthony Wilden, "Pars divers moyens."

sics that he could always draw on them for his own guidance and the enlightenment of others. In short, Michel was to be a humanist, full of the classical wisdom so fashionable at the time among some members of the court and Parlement but denied to Pierre, who read only vernacular languages with ease. A host of these humanists were at work in France— mostly turning out collections of adages and moral lessons culled from the classics with no attempt at originality. Occasionally, a history or philosophical treatise of some distinction might appear, like La Boétie's *Discourse on Voluntary Servitude.*

Pierre's adulation of men who quoted Seneca obviously prepared the way for Michel's adoration of La Boétie, who made great efforts to live like a sage and took superb advantage of the opportunity to die like one. Our detailed knowledge of La Boétie's performance on his death bed comes from the famous letter addressed by Michel to Pierre, in which he reveals himself so awed by his friend's stoic composure that he resolves to imitate it for the rest of his life. Previously, though admiring such Spartan heroes, Montaigne may have found them a bit too demanding for his easy-going nature. Now, overwhelmed and inspired by his friend's death, he tenses himself to carry the torch that has been passed to him. But the role of humanist was at best a part-time assignment, and not always compatible with some of the others he had to play.

Montaigne may have had older brothers; but if so, they died very young, making him from birth onward the heir apparent to the seigneurie. Primarily, this meant that he was expected to fill his father's shoes as head of the family and trustee of the estate. At 32, to carry out this role, he took a suitable wife, apparently selected for him by others, and begot the first of six children, only one of whom lived past infancy. And Pierre's last will exhorted him to act as a father toward his many brothers and sisters. Michel often wrote of his father's interest in improving the château (which was large enough to accommodate forty-five noble visitors and their servants on the occasion of a royal visit), and he had frequent opportunities to extend his holdings of surrounding land. Finally, he inherited a certain responsibility to the peasants of the area.

Anyone who took the role of seigneur seriously would have had to invest in it a very considerable portion of his energies. If we can trust the essays, Michel seems to have done his duty in this respect, but without much enthusiasm. He was always glad of a chance to travel and leave the estate management to someone else. An interesting aspect of his social station is that he appears, for all his intellectual independence, to have been physically dependent on a host of servants—if he were left without a cook, he wrote, he would starve. He was always attended by a valet, and often dictated to a secretary or had books read to him. Although he rode apart from his companions and ruminated while on the road, he was followed by a retinue on any long journey. Even at home, he had to retreat to his tower across the courtyard for solitude.

The role of seigneur, of course, did not fall to Michel until Pierre died (1568). For more than a decade before this, the son's chief role was that of magistrate in the Parlement of Bordeaux. The Parlement was the seat of royal power in southwestern France; and, together with its sister bodies in Paris and six other principal cities, it helped determine national policy and was often asked to ratify treaties. It registered (and sometimes balked at registering) royal edicts, thus promulgating them as law in its own area. Conflicts between national and local interests, therefore, had to be thrashed out on its floor or by its emissaries to the court, among whom Montaigne often figured. The Parlement divided itself into several chambers for the administration of justice; it decided disputes over taxes owed to the crown; and when occasion demanded it took steps to keep the peace, the members even taking arms themselves at the head of local forces.

Montaigne's activities as a magistrate combined functions we would today divide among a state attorney, a legislator, and a judge. He prepared cases for trial, debated questions of policy and security, and sat in judgment on most civil and some criminal cases. The work was hard and the hours long, but there is no evidence that Montaigne shirked it, although he appears to have taken frequent advantage of opportunities to travel to Paris, usually on a mixture of court business and his own.

If this complex role taught him to apply himself with diligence, it also taught him to distinguish his personal feelings and convictions from the requirements of the role. Venality in office was the rule at that time, and the king depended heavily on the fixed sums paid by his magistrates for the privilege of collecting fees from litigants. Montaigne speaks out in his essays against both the cost of justice, which made it unavailable to the poor, and the inequity and immense confusion of the laws themselves. Like anyone closely involved with the law, he was keenly aware that distinctions made in the name of universal justice were, in the event, often arbitrary and artificial. And he even claims to have sentenced men too lightly because the laws were full of error and the punishments so unreasonable. Observing national and local politics, too, he could not fail to be struck by the distance between principle and necessity. The humanist and the magistrate within him must have waged many a battle; and the outcome was a skeptical attitude toward institutions in general, combined with a pragmatic willingness to get the world's work done.

The roles of humanist, seigneur, and magistrate were by no means the only ones open to a young man of good birth. Many such became courtiers or diplomats, and Montaigne's frequent visits to Paris may indicate ambitions of this sort. During the years immediately following his retirement from the Parlement, when he was writing his first essays, he probably spent much time at court; and we know that he was involved in important but vain negotiations between the Catholic and Protestant leaders, Henry of Guise and Henry of Navarre (later Henry IV). The essays tell us little about what he did at court, but they comment at length on his reasons for not staying there. He was not immune to ambition, but he wanted to speak his mind rather than conceal his true opinions beneath small talk or lies. Dissimulation, Montaigne admits, is often necessary in the interests of state, but he claims that he could not bring himself to it. Writing on this subject, in fact, he seldom fails to speak metaphorically of the masks worn by courtiers to conceal their true selves. And during public ceremonies he generally felt more withdrawn than he did when alone.

Montaigne's love of bluntness favored another typically noble role: that of soldier. His father had followed the Vicomte de Lautrec to the Italian wars, exercising a privilege and a duty that would not have pertained to his bourgeois ancestors. Montaigne confirms his own status as a gentleman by embracing the military vocation in print, and shows signs of having enjoyed the soldier's life when he tried it; but that was evidently not often. If Pierre admired learning from a distance, I think it is fair to say that Michel admired valor in the same way. In this they were both representative of the French nobility at that time, clinging to its diminishing military function while competing with a better-educated bourgeoisie for administrative power.

At 48, a year after he had published Books One and Two of the *Essays*, Montaigne had a role thrust upon him that he would gladly have forgone. While traveling in Italy he was appointed Mayor of Bordeaux, an office that his father had held for two years. The mayor was regularly selected from the local nobility by the Bordeaux *jurats*, or councilmen; and in Montaigne's case, the jurats were probably prompted in their choice by persons close to the kings of France and Navarre. His election (and reelection for a rare second term) confirmed his success in the career of public service for which his father had provided both impetus and example. But nothing reveals the difference between the father and son more clearly than Michel's performance of the role, once he had accepted it. I shall not repeat here what he says at length in the essay "Of Husbanding Your Will," but it can be summed up in the term "role distance." Michel's great advantage over his father, he felt, was the ability to distinguish his self from his role, giving each its due but never risking exhaustion in the public interest as his father had. Montaigne said just this to the jurats of Bordeaux upon his installation. It was perhaps the first time that separation of identity from role had been publicly proclaimed.

If Montaigne's varied occupations seem to us no more than different aspects of a single role, we should consider that many gentlemen of his time confined themselves to only one or two of them. Householder, jurist, moralist, captain, diplomat, or political administrator—each of these was for some men a whole way of life. Although it was by no means unusual for one man to combine several of these roles in a lifetime, to do so well required great flexibility.

CHANGING ROLES

If Montaigne was cast in a diversity of roles, it is also important to note that when he began the *Essays*, he was in the process of changing roles, or of playing for the first time some for which he had been rehearsed.

He was 35 when his father died, leaving him head of the family. Although there is evidence that during the few years preceding he had shown more interest in the estate and responsibility for the family than he had done as a youth, his feelings about his new role were mixed. The sudden financial responsibility frightened him for a time into penny-pinching, and he later accused himself of failing to expand the château on the scale envisioned by Pierre. There also seems to have been some conflict with his strong-willed mother, who was reluctant to give up her authority in the household. All in all, it was a transition that challenged his self-possession. At 37 he retired from the Parlement to enjoy the full benefits of his seigneurie—in particular, the independence and solitude that it could afford him. This move was probably less a withdrawal from the world than a coming into his full estate, and as such it had far-reaching social implications.

The French nobility of Montaigne's time was in a state of crisis.[7] The principal reason for its existence as a class in former times had been the military support it furnished to the king. But its usefulness in this respect was diminishing as more and more commoners and mercenaries were employed. In public offices, nobles were being replaced by bourgeois, who were often better-educated and richer. A long period of rising prices had left the nobles land-poor, and they were prevented by law from participating in trade. True, they were exempt from most taxes; but the exemption was repeatedly attacked by resentful commoners and sometimes overlooked by the crown.

Confused about its own *raison d'être*, the nobility was also heterogeneous in membership. Perhaps as little as ten percent of the class was unquestionably of noble descent. For example, bourgeois families who acquired noble lands were by common consent "ennobled" by the third generation. Moreover, public officers, such as the members of a Parlement, were considered *nobles de robe longue* (as opposed to *robe courte*), or simply *nobles de robe* (as opposed to *nobles d'épée*). As might be expected, there was much animosity between sword and gown. If Montaigne, in his essays, seems coolly confident of his place in this ill-defined hierarchy, the appearance may have been artfully contrived. The château had been purchased

[7] My social profile of the French nobility is drawn from Bitton, *The French Nobility in Crisis.*

by his great-grandfather, but his grandfather had still continued the wine, salt fish, and dye trades to which the family owed its fortune.

Michel was the first of his line to drop the surname Eyquem and go by the name of his house alone. His career in the Parlement identified him with the *nobles de robe longue*; and though his father had borne arms for the crown, Michel's own preference for intellectual achievement made his status problematic. He wanted to belong to the nobility, but he also wanted to alter its character. Many aristocrats, particularly noble soldiers, were scornful of learning, and even illiterate; they were also violent, and in the wars of religion they openly practiced banditry and torture. It was part of Montaigne's stated program to revive *vertu* as the sustaining force of his crumbling class—to help institute an educated, humane aristocracy.

He also wanted to bring humanism out of the study and into public affairs. He had edited the works of La Boétie, and, at his father's urging, he had translated and published the lengthy *Natural Theology* of Raymond Sebond. Thus before he left the Parlement he could claim to be a man of letters; but he scorned being thought a mere "maker of books." Montaigne's model man was both wise and valorous—an ancient ideal that Pierre may have dreamed of reviving when he began to educate his son.

In the years immediately surrounding Montaigne's retirement, then, he faced a triple challenge: to make the transitions from son to father, from magistrate to gentleman, and from translator and editor to "noble sage." His intention (inspired by Pierre) to humanize the nobility and to ennoble humanism set him apart from both roles. He, Michel de Montaigne, did not quite fit any of the available social categories; he was something undeveloped, something that did yet fully exist.

PHYSICAL SYMPTOMS

All the human divisions and diversities I have discussed so far are social in nature, if we allow the term "social" to stretch from the broadest historical movements to intimate identifications of one person with another. But every instance of human development has a biological dimension as well, and the ego is challenged to integrate not only self and society but also body and mind.[8]

When Michel was 28 his father developed a kidney stone, suffering intensely for seven years until his death. This experience weighed heavily on Michel, who anticipated the same end for himself and suffered mentally from the disease for years before he felt its physical symptoms. Indeed, he later admits that the anticipation caused him greater anguish than the stone he eventually suffered from, a fact that clearly indicates the impossibility of separating bodily and mental problems. In an obvious material sense, Montaigne had received his bodily substance from his parents, together with his inescapable mortality and a possible predisposition to certain diseases. At the same time, his personal identity was largely based on his relations with his father, which involved a vast complex of social expectations and emotional interdependencies.

There was also the curious coincidence that the name of Michel's father, Pierre, is identical with the French name of the disease that killed him—*la pierre*. On an irrational and probably unconscious level, Michel may well have felt that to share in his father's identity was unavoidably to die his father's death. At least the avidity with which he fixed on the stone as his particular fate long before it had given him a single twinge would suggest that this was so. Although

[8] See Erikson, *Identity: Youth and Crisis*, pp. 73–74; *Childhood and Society*, pp. 36–38.

bodily inheritance and dietary habits may have played their part in the onset of the disease, we must admit that that onset served a psychological purpose. To avoid the kidney stone would have been in some sense to reject his father's contribution to his own life and death; to succumb to it would have been to die without living his own independent life. The task of individuation required him to accept his bodily identification with his father (and through him, with the whole mortal race) and then to transcend it. And in fact, Montaigne learned to live with the stone, and even to enjoy winning his recurrent bouts with it.

The same is true of physical energy. Pierre had been an exceptionally vigorous and active man, and was a skilled athlete even late in life. Michel, by contrast, was uncoordinated, clumsy, and above all, lazy. The great energy that is evident to us in his writing style and behavior was something that he did not know how to marshal for much of his life; and it appeared as a perpetual restlessness that was often comic, as when he bit his fingers while gobbling food too hastily. His conversation was usually too loud and too shrill, and he was known for his undiplomatic outbursts in public. He tells us that he could not sit long over a book, nor indeed anywhere but on his horse, where he boasts of remaining for ten hours a day while traveling. Obviously, the laziness that had characterized him since childhood was not a lack of vigor but a lack of will. His task was to harness his energy to purposes of his own—once again, a physical problem with a psychological solution.

Before we leave the biological level, it may be interesting to note that the disease of which Montaigne eventually died was an infection of the throat. For the last few days of his life, it is said, he was deprived of speech—he, who had once written that he valued discussion above any other action in life and would sooner be blind than deaf or dumb. The event

casts a curious light in retrospect upon his statements, made
some twenty years earlier, that he continually felt death gripping him by the throat. This congruence between metaphor
and bodily process is something I will investigate in the individual essays.

ANXIETY AND PSYCHIC INTEGRATION

The ambiguous relationship between Montaigne and his
father is reflected on the level of inner feelings as well as
physically. Michel *wanted* to fulfill his father's hopes—to cut
a figure at court, to elaborate the château, and to make a name
as a writer. Yet the attributes he most admired, so he tells us,
were idleness and freedom. In my opinion, this fundamental
conflict between his father's ambitions for him and his own
dimly sensed individuality goes far to explain the repeated
ambivalence of the early essays. Time and again in these
"immature" efforts he sets out to exercise his judgment on
military matters (his father had been a soldier), asking in
one form or another whether it is better to *faire teste*, to
stiffly oppose one's enemy, or to submit when up against
superior force. And time and again he wavers or ends in
indecision.[9]

It is amusing, too, to see this man who is supposedly so
devoted to his ease take alarm when he experiences true idleness. In I: 8 he writes that after his retirement he sought to
keep his mind occupied with writing lest it run away with
him like a wild horse. And the earliest version of I: 21 reveals how far he was, at the time he began writing, from
extending freedom to his imagination. It was a mysterious
power that was not to be trusted.

At this stage in his life, Montaigne's ambivalence was accompanied by defensiveness. He writes at length about fear,

[9] See, for example, *Essays*, I: 15, I: 45, and I: 47. The earliest version of I: 14
also expresses an ambivalence that later additions resolve.

pain, and death, as if he were trying to fend them off with words. He exaggerates his praise of the tension and heroism with which the Stoics embraced tragedy. In both of the essays just mentioned, his imagery suggests a fear of becoming fertile and productive, lest he engender "monsters." The irrational or deviant products of his imagination are either disowned or repressed. (Later, we shall see them operating on the structure of his essays with the devious but irresistible force of bodily drives, all the more powerful for their being unconscious.) And his retirement itself, whatever other excellent reasons may account for it, was also a defensive withdrawal from the world.

I said in the Introduction that ambivalence and defensiveness are signs of a failure, or at least a temporary reluctance, to face up to some challenge and the anxiety that accompanies it. Nothing could be more evident than the anxiety that threatened Montaigne in mid-career. This is not to suggest that he was neurotic. On the contrary, he was undergoing a crucial but normal stage in his development, as both Strowski and Frame have made abundantly clear. The years of his retirement were critical. If the diverse forces operating upon and within him were to be integrated, he needed time. He had somehow to make a place for pain and death in a life of physical and moral vigor, to abandon his rational defenses and face unarmed whatever monsters might live within him, to temper his judgment with a liberated imagination. The bodily and mental aspects of his experience, as well as the physical inheritance, irrational attachments, and social expectations bequeathed him by those he loved, had to be subsumed in a viable ego identity. And as he discovered his own complex dimensions, he had to confront anxiety with the courage to become more actively and openly himself.

How was all this to be accomplished? Human history displays an almost infinite variety of ways in which men can respond to the threat of disintegration. All of them, if they are successful, involve *work*—effort that sets out to construct a world more suited to one's self or a self more adequate to the world, and always, in the event, alters both. Montaigne's chosen work was writing; and the next chapter will briefly sketch his growth as a writer and the process by which the essays came to embody his personal development.

2. The Text as Self-Image

It is not difficult to see what led Montaigne to write. His education had, from the first, acquainted him with the best ancient authors, and he saw through the pedantry with which others surrounded them because they were already his intimate friends. At 33, well before he began the *Essays*, he gave evidence of a keen interest in the literary craft, making judicious critical notes on some of the books he read. His translation of Sebond, finished when he was 35 but begun, perhaps, some 15 years earlier, ran to almost a thousand pages and displayed considerable skill.[1] And his edition of La Boétie, besides perpetuating his friend's name, did some credit to his own, for it was he who wrote the elegant dedications to important men.

When retirement at 37 left Montaigne free to be a full-time gentleman, he may have hoped for recognition as a *bel esprit* —a person of some intellectual brilliance—or at the very least as an *honnête homme* to whom writing was an avocational ornament. The form in which he began to set down his thoughts was well suited to this purpose: it was easy, requir-

[1] Trinquet, *La Jeunesse de Montaigne*, pp. 579-81.

ing no sustained effort and allowing him to choose his own time, topic, and approach; it was informal, or could easily be made to seem so; and it was modeled on the many eclectic books produced by other aristocrats of his era. Despite his protestations to the contrary, Montaigne's writing was probably worked and polished. Most critics agree that the *Essays'* apparent spontaneity is deceptive; and even after it had been achieved, he continued to edit his text with great attention to detail. Although he may have written diffidently at the beginning, it seems clear that by his early forties, when he undertook the "Apology for Raymond Sebond," he fully intended to publish his work.

But although writing was an absorbing craft and a desirable social goal, Montaigne did not immediately discover what he had to say. The earliest essays were tentative "tryouts" (*essais*) of his judgment, inconsequential except for the evidence they give us of his psychological and stylistic starting point. Let us look at the first version of I: 12, "Of Constancy," a typical example short enough to be quoted in its entirety.

▲ The precepts of resoluteness and constancy do not state that we must not protect ourselves as much as it lies in our power from the evils and troubles that threaten us; nor consequently that we should not fear being taken by surprise. On the contrary, all honorable means of safeguarding ourselves from evils are not only permitted but laudable. And constancy's part is played principally in bearing troubles patiently and with a firm stance where there is no remedy. So that there is neither any bodily suppleness, nor any move with hand weapons, that we should despise if it serves to safeguard us from the blow that is struck at us.

However, in cannonades, once you are in the line of fire, as the chances of war often bring about, it is unbecoming to move because of the threat of the shot, inasmuch as because of its violence and speed we consider it unavoidable. And there is many a one who, for having either lifted his hand or ducked his head, has at least given a laugh to his companions.

Yet in the campaign Emperor Charles V made against us in

Provence, the marquis de Guast, on his way to reconnoiter the city of Arles, having emerged from the shelter of a windmill under cover of which he had approached, was spotted by the seigneur de Bonneval and the seneschal d'Agenois, who were walking on top of the city's amphitheater. They pointed him out to the seigneur de Villiers, head of the artillery, who aimed a culverin so accurately that if the said marquis, seeing the match applied, had not sprung aside, it was thought that he would have got it in the body. And likewise a few years before, Lorenzo de' Medici, duke of Urbino and father of the Queen Mother, besieging Mondolfo, a place in Italy in the territories that they call the Vicariate, seeing the match applied to a piece that pointed right at him, did well to duck; for otherwise the shot, which only grazed the top of his head, would undoubtedly have hit him in the stomach.

To tell the truth about it, I do not think that these movements are deliberate; for how can you judge whether the aim is high or low in such a sudden thing? It is much easier to believe that fortune favored their fright, and that another time this would be just as good a way to jump into the shot as to avoid it. (*DB*/I, pp. 28–29; *S*, pp. 30–31.)

The brevity of this essay makes its structure particularly clear: "The law of constancy says one thing, *but* practice often indicates the contrary; *nevertheless*, here are two examples (one from the *Mémoires* of the frères du Bellay, another from Guicciardini's *History of Italy*) in support of my opening statement; *but to tell the truth*, I believe it's all a matter of luck." Among the essays composed between 1572 and 1574, there are some much longer and more impressive than this, but they do not differ greatly from it in method of composition. Villey's well-chosen term for these early efforts is *essais impersonnels*. They focus our attention not on Montaigne the author but on the ideas and examples to which he himself is attending. Those dealing with moral principles might perhaps have direct application to his life, but they are couched in very general terms. Those dealing with military affairs share the weakness of any armchair strategy: the author is obviously a dilettante who in this case does not even ask us to take him seriously or attend to him for more than a few pages at a time.

The very triviality of the early essays makes them interesting in the light of Montaigne's later accomplishments. We who know that beneath this diffidence sleeps a literary giant can read in them things of which he himself must have been unaware. For instance, the author's preoccupation with fear and defense, his ambivalent feelings about self-assertion, and his tendency to favor skeptical conclusions all betray a divided and anxious man. As I suggested in Chapter One, Montaigne at this point needs to establish a firmer identity; and as he continues to write we can see how he is able to do so.

First, he writes longer essays about subjects that do touch on his own experience: death, disease, custom, law, solitude, inconsistency, and so on. Such topics inevitably elicit personal reflections and anecdotes, and aspects of his subjective life emerge from his former "objectivity." By 1574, two years after beginning, he has written several essays of this kind, although he is probably still producing some of the short, impersonal type, which will be published later. In the following six years, he becomes far more openly concerned with himself, not only discussing his experiences and his character, but sometimes even commenting on the business of writing in which he is engaged. The *essais personnels* of this kind that I will discuss in Chapters Six through Eight were all begun between 1578 and 1580, the year in which Books One and Two of the *Essays* at last went to press.

The second means by which Montaigne's self-portrait develops is more complex and individual. Once his book is printed he continues to write new essays, which will eventually be published as Book Three; but he also reworks the old essays extensively. Sometimes he alters a word or a phrase, often he inserts an appropriate quotation from his current reading, and not infrequently he adds an important passage that develops or even contradicts a point previously made. By the time the three books of essays are published together in 1588, Books One and Two contain some six hundred additions. Nor does he stop there. After 1588, he writes no new essays, but he fills the margins of his own copy with additions that will amount to one-fourth of the book's total length when it is posthumously republished in 1595 (under a new and appropriate epigraph: "He acquires strength as he goes").

It is thus possible to distinguish three "layers" of composition in Books One and Two, and two in Book Three. Recent editors identify every passage in Montaigne's text by a letter *A*, *B*, or *C*, in superscript or parentheses, to tell us whether the words first appeared in 1580, 1588, or 1595, respectively. (Very minor corrections made in the editions of 1582 and 1587 are not indicated separately.) There are obvious general differences between the three versions, some quite substantial.

Version *A* spans the eight crucial years of Montaigne's self-discovery and maturation. Grouped according to dates of composition,[2] the *A* essays show us several stages of this development. At first he is imitative, hesitant, and impersonal, then more inclined to discuss himself but still fearful and somewhat rigid. Later, under the influence of Sextus Empiricus (principally, of course, in the "Apology"), he becomes sweepingly skeptical. And finally he is confident of his powers and eager to talk about himself, though careful not to appear immodest.

Version *B*, which includes the entire initial version of Book Three, shows Montaigne's clear determination to make his book a self-portrait. The warm public reception given his first edition, his travel in foreign lands, and his two successful terms as mayor encourage him to be even bolder and more original. Nevertheless, many of the early essays are not greatly altered in this version. He lets them stand partly as

[2] The dates have been roughly established by Villey, I, 347–403.

evidence of his own diversity, which is a major theme of the work as a whole, and partly, one suspects, because he has not yet rethought the subjects with which some of them deal. At any rate, the additions to Books One and Two seem to lag behind Book Three in revealing the salient aspects of his development. As we shall see in a number of cases, *B* additions often do no more than reinforce earlier arguments, as if Montaigne were being carried along mostly by inertia.

C additions, by contrast, often show a complete change in direction, a general revision of earlier attitudes. They are by no means uniform in mood; on the contrary, they range from occasional depression through wry detachment to a mellow serenity. But they persistently clarify self-descriptive observations that Montaigne has only hinted at in the *B* text.

Montaigne's self-image consists in about equal measure of comments on himself and responses to the world, mingled just as they are in the ongoing consciousness of daily life. Projected into the medium of written words, this image is far more useful to him than any estimation of himself gained only from memory and fleeting self-perception. He is able to lay out a variety of perspectives on himself at the same time, to analyze and compare separate moments of his existence, to avoid complete submersion in each successive mood or concern, and to observe that the forces tugging him this way and that have a common center in his ego, which can keep them in balance. His psychic integration is essentially an understanding achieved by constructing an image of himself that can be studied and observed as the ego cannot.

But even if we accept that Montaigne's essays are essentially his composite self-image, it is no simple matter to unfold that image for study. For one thing, it is an image of change, and we must translate its spatial arrangement back into temporal terms. There are several possible ways to do this, and each yields a different result. Villey has shown us with remarkable thoroughness how the essays develop *as a whole*, and all sub-

sequent critics are dependent on his achievement in sorting
out the chronological sequence of the chapters and their accretions. In a different way, Frame has compared the separate
strata of composition in order to arrive at a picture of *the
author's* overall development.[3] His conclusions, though convincing and helpful, seem to lack two things with which we
can hope to supplement them. The first, as I indicated in the
Introduction, is an explicit reference to psychological principles—not to supplant but to enrich the traditional categories of biographical understanding. The second is an analysis of the internal development of *individual essays*. Such an
approach both sharpens our appreciation of specific passages
and broadens our understanding of the creative process as it
works in Montaigne's mind.

It is important to know, for example (as Frame, building
on Villey, has told us), that between 1580 and 1588 Montaigne became much less critical of the common people,
whom he had previously regarded with some of the humanists' traditional scorn, and that after 1588 he went so far as
to identify himself with all men, no matter how common:
"Nous sommes tous du vulgaire."[4] But general observations
of this sort, valid as they are, are of little help in understanding specific anomalies, such as Montaigne's rejection of his
family and servants in the *C* additions to II: 8. These we
must examine in terms of their position in that particular
essay, where the author's literary success is counterbalanced
by the frustration of more intimate emotional aims, and
where he moves progressively toward the use of literature as
an escape from humanity rather than a link with it.

To give another example, critics have not altogether ig-
nored Montaigne's reaction against rigid standards for trustworthy evidence, which appears in version *C* toward the end

[3] Frame, *Montaigne's Discovery of Man.*

[4] See Frame, *Montaigne: A Biography*, pp. 300–302.

of I: 21. But no one I recall has pointed out the relation of this passage to imagination,[5] which is the subject of the essay, nor traced the progress of free association in the essay's three successive texts. Such a procedure, I hope to show, can throw light on most of Montaigne's seeming non sequiturs, revealing the movements by which each essay grew and adding much detail to our picture of how the man developed.

Sometimes Montaigne amends an essay because he has changed since he first wrote it and wants to record the difference. At other times, rereading his text, he observes something he had not previously seen, and the essay changes him, eliciting a new reaction. Often, of course, we cannot tell which process is at work, and must simply note that book and man change together. But the two directions of interpretive movement—from the man to the work and from the work to the man—should be kept in mind, because ultimately my subject is the *distance* between the author, his Self, and the literary image that reflects them both. Montaigne uses his writing to help him form a clear and articulated idea of his Self, and we have already seen many of his reasons for doing so. But he also uses it to try to compensate for the feeling of being separated from himself. This second attempt is another phase of the dialectic I have been describing, a phase that ends only with his death.

To demonstrate Montaigne's starting point, I have already quoted one essay in its earliest version. To show how he and his book interact, I shall in each of the next six chapters examine an essay begun before 1580, amended in 1588, and enlarged again after that date.

[5] A relation suggested to me by Harry Berger, Jr.

3. *"That to Philosophize Is to Learn to Die"*

"ᴬ With such frequent and ordinary examples passing before our eyes, how can we possibly rid ourselves of the thought of death and of the idea that at every moment it is gripping us by the throat?" (I: 20. *DB/I*, p. 57; *OC*, p. 84; *S*, p. 59.) So Montaigne wrote in the earliest version of the essay. But his fear of death is suspect. It takes more than the sight of corpses to make us afraid, just as it takes more than a reasonable argument to reassure us. Philosophic counsel is of little use in this matter because the experience goes deeper than reason: it is a particular form of our general anxiety about the "nothingness" that is part and parcel of human existence.

Of course, a concrete encounter with death can provide generalized anxiety with an object or can aggravate an already habitual fear. The second case seems to apply to Montaigne, if, as he tells us, his mind had indeed dwelt on death even in his lustiest youth. The loss of La Boétie and of his father (not to mention those of a brother and a daughter) must have intensified his morbid state of mind, and also forced him to consider what he was to do with the remainder of his life.

As he tells us elsewhere, La Boétie's death was especially unfortunate because it cut off a career of enormous promise. Each had foreseen great things for the other, and Montaigne was left, so to speak, to carry on for both of them. Pierre's expectations for his son, if less clearly formulated, had been even more compelling: we can fairly say that Michel was assigned the role of a distinguished intellectual from the moment he was weaned; in addition, his father's death left Michel heir to the seigneurie, with all that this entailed of both status and responsibility.

Any father's death, or any friend's, will normally lead offspring and friends to reflect on mortality, and it is scarcely surprising to find Montaigne, so soon after his double loss, pondering the question of how to die. But I am struck by the extent to which, in this essay, his preoccupation with death allows him to evade the question of how to live. In this he is aided by the Stoic precepts of La Boétie. Constant premeditation of death will allow him to get through what remains of life "without disturbance and fever" (*DB*/I, p. 62; *OC*, p. 88; *S*, p. 63). It will also prevent him from becoming too attached to his projects or too involved with other men: "‘We must . . . take especial care to have only ourselves to deal with then; for we shall have enough trouble without adding any" (*DB*/I, p. 60; *OC*, pp. 86–87; *S*, p. 61).

All this even though he may well live another 39 years (*DB*/I, p. 55; *OC*, p. 82; *S*, p. 58), and though he has yet to fulfill most of the expectations held for him by his best friend, by his father, or (allowing for some ambivalence) by himself. It is a classic example of bad faith. At the moment when his future life becomes most acutely problematic and challenging, Montaigne fixes his attention on death and resolves to keep it there. It will be my task to show how, in the process of writing and rewriting the essay on death (I: 20), he penetrated and dissolved this self-deception.

The earliest text of the essay, first published in 1580 but largely composed in 1572,[1] consists of a fairly orderly argument in four sections. The first point made is that we cannot be happy until we have found a remedy against the fear of death; thus the prime duty of philosophy (as Cicero had said, and Socrates before him) is "to teach us to die." The second section rejects the alternative course, which is to forget about death until the moment it arrives. Such nonchalance is possible only for those too ignorant to realize that death can strike at any time. When it catches them unprepared, "what torments, what cries, what frenzy, what despair overwhelms them!" To avoid ultimate panic we must think continually about death; this is the third and principal point. The remainder of the essay puts this advice into practice by collecting philosophers' opinions on the subject, especially those of Lucretius and Seneca.

The typically Roman stance toward death, which Montaigne so admires, displays an obvious contradiction: the aim of philosophy is contentment and tranquillity, but that goal is to be attained by an unrelenting tension. To assure our peace of mind, we must continually ward off the enemy:

᷄ Let us learn to meet it steadfastly and to combat it.... Let us tense ourselves and make an effort. Amid feasting and gaiety let us ever keep in mind this refrain, the memory of our condition; and let us never allow ourselves to be so carried away by pleasure that we do not sometimes remember in how many ways this happiness of ours is a prey to death, and how death's clutches threaten it. (*DB*/I, pp. 58–59; *OC*, p. 85; *S*, p. 60.)

But even as his exhortation rises to a climax, Montaigne hints at what he will later frankly admit: that such rigid invulnerability is inhuman.

᷄ The body, when bent and bowed, has less strength to support a burden, and so has the soul; we must raise and strengthen her

[1] Villey, I, 353–54.

34

against the assault of this adversary. For as it is impossible for the soul to be at rest while she fears death, so, if she can gain assurance against it, she can boast of a thing *as it were beyond man's estate*: that it is impossible for worry, torment, fear, or even the slightest displeasure to dwell in her. She is made mistress of her passions and lusts, mistress over indigence, shame, poverty, and all other wounds of fortune. Let us gain this advantage, *those of us who can*: this is the true and sovereign liberty, which enables us to thumb our noses [*faire la figue*] at force and injustice and to laugh [*nous mocquer*] at prisons and chains. (*DB*/I, p. 63; *OC*, pp. 89–90; *S*, pp. 63–64. My italics.)

The use of the first person plural in both passages has a pathetic ring. Not only does Montaigne avoid the personal commitment that goes with saying "I," but also, by phrasing the whole thing as an exhortation, he places its fulfillment in an indefinite and probably unattainable future. It is all too obvious that this sublime discipline, although he may have attempted it, has not rewarded him with freedom from care. What he calls liberty is in fact defiance, expressed by a slightly obscene and mocking gesture.

There are other things worth noting about this moral posture. The first is that although Montaigne calls on Christianity to support his pose of "contempt for life," he quite overlooks the complementary aspect of Pauline asceticism, which is the assurance of victory over death. Rather, he takes his inspiration from Horace, to whom death is an implacable predator breathing down our necks:

> ▲ As surely it pursues the man that flees,
> Nor does it spare the haunches slack
> Of warless youth, or its timid back.
> (*DB*/I, p. 58; *OC*, p. 84; *S*, p. 60.)

This image had found its way into Christian art during late medieval times, as witnessed by the popular scenes of the Dance of Death, numerous examples of which would have

35

been available to Montaigne. Holbein's famous woodcut "Death and the Knight"[2] epitomizes the tradition, and could easily illustrate a similar passage in another essay (I: 14) contemporary with this one:

> [A] Even as the enemy grows rougher at our flight, so pain waxes proud to see us tremble beneath it. It will make itself far easier to deal with to those who stand up against it [*luy fera teste*]. We must resist it and tense ourselves against it. By turning tail [*en nous acculant*] and retreating we call upon us the ruin that threatens us. (*DB*/I, p. 38; *OC*, p. 58; *S*, p. 39.)[3]

This brings us to a second point about Montaigne's "posture." If Death is assaulting him from behind, his problem is, metaphorically, one of anal defense. Erikson has shown how this metaphor is grounded in the physical and emotional development of children, and what a large role it played in the life of Luther.[4] Montaigne, who is in so many ways at the opposite pole of the sixteenth century from Luther, could only reach that position, it seems, by testing and eventually transcending Luther's favored mode of combat. As we shall see again and again, the crisis of his middle years was, in one respect, an anal crisis; and at the time he wrote this essay he was inclined to *faire la figue à la force*.[5]

He was also inclined to fortify his defenses with ample quotations from ancient authors, at length distending some of the essays in a manner suggestive of Luther's cramming his belly

---

[2] Reproduced from Francis Douce and Thomas Frognall Dibdin, *The Dance of Death and Holbein's Bible Cuts* (London, 1896), Plate XXX. See also Emile Mâle, *L'Art religieux de la fin du moyen age en France*, 5th ed. (Paris: Colin, 1949), pp. 347–89.

[3] For further occurrences of this image in the *Essays*, see *OC*, pp. 84, 95–96, 333, 352–53; *S*, pp. 59–60, 69, 253–54, 269.

[4] *Childhood and Society*, pp. 80–85; *Young Man Luther*, pp. 244–50.

[5] The origin of the term "faire la figue" is not entirely certain, but Littré gives as one of its meanings, "to force an enemy to eat from the anus of a mule."

The Knight

with food. Villey has pointed out that the final section of this essay (beginning at *DB*/I, p. 63; *OC*, p. 90; *S*, p. 64) is almost superfluous and may well have been added as an afterthought previous to the first publication.[6] It is a compilation of rational arguments ostensibly allaying the fear of death, but actually keeping Montaigne's attention focused on it, reinforcing rather than relieving his anxiety.

The same is true of most of the *B* (1588) additions to the essay. Apart from one passage comparing advancing age to a slow, hard death (*OC*, p. 89; *S*, p. 63), there are a score of borrowings from Roman sources, together with an emphatic development of the image of attack and defense:

> [B] But since that cannot be, since it catches you just the same, whether you flee like a coward or act like a man—[here follow the three lines from Horace quoted above]—and since no kind of armor protects you—
>
> > Hide as he will, cautious, in steel and brass,
> > Still death will drag his head outside at last.
> > (*OC*, pp. 84–85; *S*, pp. 59–60.)

Not until version *C* (posthumously published) does Montaigne recognize the connection between his defensiveness and his passion for stuffing his book with additional scraps he has collected:

> [A] And there is nothing that I investigate so eagerly as the death of men: what words, what look, what bearing they maintained at that time; nor is there a place in the histories that I note so attentively. [C] This shows in the abundance [*la farcissure*—literally, "stuffing"] of my illustrative examples; I have indeed a particular fondness for this subject. If I were a maker of books, I would make a register, with comments, of various deaths. (*OC*, p. 88; *S*, p. 62.)

But he goes right on collecting and quoting, and even adds some quibbles of his own:

[6] Villey, I, 303.

°You are in death while you are in life; for you are after death when you are no longer in life. Or, if you prefer it this way, you are dead after life; but during life you are dying; and death affects the dying much more roughly than the dead, and more keenly and essentially. (*OC*, p. 91; *S*, p. 65.)

°It does not concern you dead or alive: alive, because you are; dead, because you are no more. (*OC*, p. 93; *S*, p. 66.)

By this time, Montaigne is no longer trying to ward off death, nor even to ignore it; he is playing with it, and cheerfully deprecating the examples he has collected by calling them "farcissure." Let us look at other ways in which the third version of the essay transforms its earlier content.

Perhaps the most obvious change is that Montaigne weakens his reference to the Christian "contempt for life" by adding forceful remarks on "contempt for death." In place of a sentence in which he despaired of reaching a state of contentment that would protect him from the fear of death (*DB*/I, p. 54), he substitutes a paragraph ending with this assertion: "°Now among the principal benefits of virtue is disdain for death, a means that furnishes our life with a soft tranquillity" (*OC*, p. 81; *S*, p. 57). Defensive premeditation now gives way to nonchalance, a quality previously scorned as "brutish" (*OC*, p. 84; *S*, p. 59). Immediately following his climactic statement on Stoic invulnerability, Montaigne visibly relaxes: "°What does it matter [*que chaut-il*] when it [death] comes, since it is inevitable?" (*OC*, p. 90; *S*, p. 64).

The ideal of contentment itself is thoroughly reinterpreted. No sooner has Montaigne used the word, in the first paragraph of the essay, than he digresses at length in order to show that the means to contentment is not austerity, but a vigorous pursuit of pleasure. "°Whatever they say, in virtue itself the ultimate goal we aim at is voluptuousness" (*OC*, p. 80; *S*, p. 56). This interpolation and the many others that follow affect the form of the essay as much as its content. In place of an orderly argument that keeps our attention focused on the threat of death, we have the "uneven, irregular, and multiform movement" that Montaigne elsewhere (III: 3) ascribes to life itself (*OC*, p. 796; *S*, p. 621).

Yet another revealing theme is touched on in Montaigne's digression: that of masks and roles. This metaphor was already present in the 1580 version, where the stages of life were likened to the passing seasons, and those in turn to Nature's role in an eternal comedy (*DB/I*, p. 64; *OC*, p. 92; *S*, pp. 65–66). The essay ended with the hope that by stripping death of its frightful mask and funereal trappings, we might find it to be a friend (*DB/I*, pp. 65–66; *OC*, pp. 94–95; *S*, p. 68). The preceding essay (I: 19), closely linked to this one by topic, position, and date of composition,[7] had observed that in the last act of life's comedy our philosophic mask will be ripped off, and our composure may prove to have been feigned.

To this admission that philosophy is but a role, Montaigne now adds an interesting refinement. Speaking of disagreements among philosophic sects, he writes: "°But whatever role [*personnage*] man undertakes to play, he always plays his own at the same time" (*OC*, p. 80; *S*, p. 56). The line implies that even while sporting the Stoic mask he himself had been pursuing not the Stoics' version of the Good, but a more universally human one. Now, speaking for himself, he identifies Good with Pleasure. "°I like to beat their ears with that word, which so goes against their grain.... This voluptuousness, for being more lusty, sinewy, robust, and manly, is only the more seriously voluptuous" (*Ibid.*).

Perhaps the most striking contrast between the first and last versions of the essay involves the introduction of an entirely new metaphor, *la couvade*. The verb *couver* derives from the Latin *cubare*, to lie down, and is used of birds that

[7] Villey, I, 353.

sit on their eggs to hatch them. It indicates a posture, therefore, diametrically opposed to that of the knight in mortal
combat, whose stance Montaigne describes by the idiom *faire
teste*. The brooding, feminine mode of *la couvade* is now used
to describe the very process of premeditation that formerly
involved so much discipline and tension. "⁰ Since I am constantly brooding [*me couve*] over my thoughts and settling
them within me [*les couche en moy*], I am at all times about
as well prepared as I can be. And the coming of death will
teach me nothing new" (*OC*, p. 86; *S*, p. 61).

Certain of the shifts I have been noting—from masculine
to feminine metaphors and from defensive to playful attitudes—indicate that Montaigne's imagination is progressively
supplementing his judgment as a means of responding to the
fear of death. Unlike judgment, which tends to fix our attention on a problem and hold it there, imagination unpredict-
ably metamorphoses the object of our concern or diverts our
attention to other matters entirely. Imaginative freedom may
be either constructive or alarming. A good case in point is the
use of impersonation in this essay. When Montaigne first employed it, in version *A*, it served to intensify his fear:

ᴬ I was born on the last day of February, 1533; it was only just
two weeks ago that I passed the age of thirty-nine years, and I need
at least that many more. But to be bothered meanwhile by the
thought of a thing so far off would be folly. After all, young and
old think about it equally little. And there is no man so decrepit
that as long as he sees Methuselah ahead of him, he does not think
he has another year left in his body. Furthermore, poor fool that
you are, who has assured you the term of your life? You are building on the tales of doctors. Look rather at facts and experience. By
the ordinary run of things, you have been living a long time now
by extraordinary favor; you have passed the accustomed limits of
life; and to prove this, count how many more of your acquaintances have died before your age than have attained it; and even
of those who have glorified their lives by renown, make a list, and

I'll wager I'll find more of them who died before thirty-five than after. (*DB*/I, pp. 55–56; *OC*, pp. 82–83; *S*, p. 58.)

Here is Montaigne chatting with us about the hour of his birth and the follies of the aged, when suddenly a stern and contemptuous voice intrudes: "Dauantage, pauure fol que tu es. . . ." The use of direct address has more force in Montaigne than it might have in another writer because, as Strowski tells us, he wrote to be read aloud.[8] This moment is therefore a dramatic event. The author has suddenly donned a mask and is impersonating—whom? Methuselah? Seneca? The *ennemy* and *adversaire* who pursues us in the verses of Horace and in the Dance of Death? Overtones of all these are present; and the effect is chilling when, abandoning the easy distance established in the preceding lines between speaker (*je*) and reader (*vous*), Montaigne abruptly closes in on us with the intimate and overbearing *tu*.

Later in version *A* Montaigne resorts once more to impersonation: "But nature forces us to it. 'Go out of this world,' she says, 'as you entered it.' " And so on for a page and a half of philosophic consolations, ending thus: " 'A thousand men, a thousand animals, and a thousand other creatures die at the very moment when you die.' Such are the good counsels of our mother Nature" (*DB*/I, pp. 64–65; *OC*, pp. 91–94; *S*, pp. 64–65, 67). Whereas the paternal figure of threatening death was used to intensify our fear, the figure of mother Nature is used to calm and reassure us. But she is somewhat less than convincing in version *A*, for her arguments are scattered and eclectic, trying to make up by cumulation what they lack in cogency. That Montaigne became increasingly sensitive to the inadequacy of this allegorical personage—carved, as it were, out of classical marble—is evidenced by the additions he made to her speech in version *C*.

---

[8] Strowski, p. 10.

° Why do you recoil, if you cannot draw back? You [*vous*] have seen enough men who were better off for dying, thereby avoiding great miseries. Have you found any man that was worse off? How simple-minded it is to condemn a thing that you have not experienced yourself or through anyone else. Why do you [*tu*] complain of me and of destiny? Do we wrong you? Is it for you to govern us, or us you? Though your age is not full-grown, your life is. A little man is a whole man, just like a big one. Neither men nor their lives are measured by the ell. (*OC*, p. 93; *S*, p. 67.)

Once again we see the movement from the relatively formal *vous* to the intimate *tu*.[9] The moderate distance between speaker and listener suddenly collapses, and Nature approaches very close. The effect, of course, is the opposite of that inspired by the "closing in" of Death. Nature is revealed as an authoritative but kindly woman: she begins by scolding, but ends by admiring this "little man" whose life is complete, regardless of his age. The movement on her part from *vous* to *tu* is balanced by the man's movement from withdrawal (*reculez-vous*) to self-confidence (*achevé ... homme entier*).

To understand the function of this imaginative impersonation in Montaigne's development, we must remind ourselves that these passages are the exteriorization of an inner dialogue, which is a curious process: the ego assumes its usual role of "I" in order to address its "me"; then, attributing to its "me" the words just spoken, it responds to them, sometimes verbally. Imagination allows the ego thus to identify with its Self, and, leaping across the distance between one position and another, to play all the parts in this intrapsychic drama. Now, fear of death is likewise the work of imagination. An ego can have no knowledge of its own death; it can only envision its Self as a lifeless object.

[9] It might be supposed that the use of *tu* here is merely a carryover from the letters of Seneca, from which Montaigne borrowed many of the arguments expressed in these passages. But in Seneca the second person singular

The ability of the ego to identify with that object has recurrently filled Montaigne with fear, and the technique he finally evolves for coping with this fear is to free his imagination for other leaps, to project himself to other vantage points. If he can identify with others and with his Self, he can identify with Death, and then with Nature. And if the distance between ego and Death seems uncomfortably small and that between ego and Nature too great, he can instantly narrow the latter gap by addressing himself as *tu*, since inner space is almost infinitely flexible. By impersonating both of these paradoxical aspects of existence, Montaigne can comprehend the truth: that his life, though utterly contingent, is also miraculously supported.

Imaginative play is one method of dealing with the terrors of one's existence. By further exteriorizing that play into literary form, Montaigne not only escapes fear but also achieves the self-actualization that he had once shrunk from undertaking. At 39 he had almost despaired of a future and had worried about fulfilling his responsibilities:

ᴬ Every minute I seem to be slipping away from myself.... To finish what I have to do before I die, even if it were one hour's work, any leisure seems short to me. Someone, looking through my tablets the other day, found a memorandum about something I wanted done after my death. I told him what was true, that although only a league away from my house, and hale and hearty, I had hastened to write it there, since I could not be certain of reaching home. (*DB*/I, p. 60; *OC*, p. 86; *S*, p. 61.)

What he either avoided seeing or lacked the courage to say was that the one thing he "had to do" above all was write these essays. It was by exercising his power to articulate—if not to overcome—the distance between life and death that

is used by the *author* to address his correspondent, whereas in Montaigne it seems to be spoken by Death and Nature to someone abjectly or resentfully dependent upon them. Compare Seneca, *Epistulae Morales*, XCIII, par. 2, with *OC*, p. 93.

he could come to terms with anxiety. It was by objectifying his inner processes that he could grasp their coherence as a Self and could make himself known to others.

The necessary limits on such a project will emerge as we proceed. But we should not overlook the evidence of its relative success that appears in this essay. The words I have quoted from the final addition of version *C* seem to dispel for once and all Montaigne's fear that death may find him lacking: "Though your age is not full-grown, your life is. A little man is a whole man, just like a big one" (*OC*, p. 93; *S*, p. 67).

4. *"Of the Power of the Imagination"*

"ᴬ I am one of those who are very much affected by apprehension; everyone is struck by it, but some are transformed" (*DB*/I, p. 66; much altered in *OC*, p. 95; *S*, p. 68). Montaigne, the champion of inconstancy, afraid of being changed! It seems hard to believe, yet this is clearly what he tells us in the opening section of this essay (I: 21. We are dealing, it must be emphasized, with the original text of 1580). Imagination, he claims, can of itself bring on disease and death. In Gallus Vibius it produced madness; criminals have died of fear before their execution; and even the ecstasies and levitations that imagination gave to the saints seem sinister. But these are indirect, and for Montaigne unlikely, results of imaginative license. He is as far from fear of the hangman as he is from a mystical trance. What really frightens him is mental freedom.

Indeed, he says as much in I: 8, describing his mind as a "runaway horse" in the "vague field of imagination." There he says it is his purpose in writing to tie his thoughts down to some subject, or at least to articulate his fantasies so that he can learn to be ashamed of them (*DB*/I, pp. 18–19; *OC*, pp. 33–34; *S*, pp. 20–21). And many of these fantasies, it would appear, are sexual. In I: 21 he gives several examples of women changed into men, and describes the action of imagination itself as an ambiguous blend of murderous assault, rape, and wet dream:

> ▲ We drip with sweat, we tremble, we turn pale and turn red at the blows of our imagination; reclining in our feather beds we feel our bodies agitated by their impact, sometimes to the point of expiring. And boiling youth, fast asleep, grows so hot in the harness that in dreams it satisfies its amorous desires. (*DB*/I, p. 67; *OC*, p. 96; *S*, p. 69.)

The freedom of our imaginations is especially evident—and therefore especially alarming—in areas like sex, where our thoughts often run counter to social taboos. Sex is also the area where imagination can be most inhibiting, as Montaigne knows "from experience." The second section of the essay, therefore, deals with impotence.

It was fashionable for gentlemen of the time to talk about (and perhaps to experience) a sudden incapacity to consummate marriage.[1] Montaigne's diagnosis is simple: impotence results from excessive tension, and tension from fear; and the only remedy for fear is diversion. One must turn one's thoughts elsewhere, or at least be persuaded that some magic remedy is available. In short, one must combat imagination with its own weapons, as Montaigne does in his essay on death.

There now follows the kernel of the essay—the seed from which it grew, as the text makes clear.[2] Montaigne here emphasizes the therapeutic power of imagination—its capacity, upon which doctors rely so heavily, for "counterenchant-

---

[1] See *OC*, p. 97, Note 5, for a discussion of this malady and its appearance in the literature of the period.

[2] "Et tout ce caprice m'est tombé presentement en main sur le conte que me faisoit un apotiquaire de feu mon pere" (*DB*/I, pp. 69–70). Inasmuch as this appears in the 1580 edition, it cannot refer, as Frame suggests (*S*, p. 74n), to an anecdote added after 1588, but must refer to the essay as a whole.

ment," for cure by faith or fantasy. He must find the anecdote he tells here especially appealing, since it concerns a remedy for *la pierre*, the disease that has killed his father and may yet kill Montaigne himself.

▲ And this whole caprice has just come to hand apropos of the story that an apothecary of my late father used to tell me, a simple man and Swiss, of a nation little addicted to vanity and lying. He had long known a merchant at Toulouse, sickly and subject to the stone, who often needed enemas, and ordered various kinds from his doctors according to the circumstances of his illness. Once they were brought to him, nothing was omitted of the accustomed formalities; often he tested them by hand to make sure they were not too hot. There he was, lying on his stomach, and all the motions were gone through—except that no injection was made. After this ceremony, the apothecary having retired and the patient being accommodated as if he had really taken the enema, he felt the same effect from it as those who do take them. And if the doctor did not find its operation sufficient, he would give him two or three more, of the same sort. My witness swears that when to save the expense (for he paid for them as if he had taken them) this sick man's wife sometimes tried to have just warm water used, the effect revealed the fraud; and having found that kind useless, they were obliged to return to the first method. (*DB*/I, pp. 69–70; *OC*, p. 102; *S*, p. 74.)

I pointed out in Chapter Three that Montaigne's mode of response to anxiety was "anal-retentive." That is, he "tightened up" and "held on" even while stuffing his mind with advice. His psychic malady was thus superficially analogous to the physical ailment that had killed his father, a urethral retention caused by stones in the bladder.[3] The analogy between anal and urethral retention (or the occurrence of both) in the merchant of Toulouse was perhaps what prompted his physicians to prescribe enemas for his relief. And the analogy

---

[3] See Erikson, *Childhood and Society*, pp. 81–83, for the connection of anal, urethral, and psychic retentiveness.

between physical and psychic retention is what prompts Montaigne to tell this tale of an enema when he wants to show that our mind is capable of curing itself. But the connection is more than a simple analogy. It is a fact that our bodies and our minds develop together, that our psyches and our muscles interpenetrate, that in the last analysis they are the same being seen from different perspectives. This is the truth underlying Erikson's theory of organ modes. It is also the truth grasped by Montaigne in the sentence that summarizes this section of his essay: "^A But all this may be attributed to the fact that the mind and the body are tightly sewn together, communicating their experience to one another" (*DB/I*, p. 71; *OC*, p. 103; *S*, p. 74. My translation).

The entire essay may be taken as a reflection on this fact, which is normally veiled from Western awareness by our habit of distinguishing body from soul. Montaigne makes the distinction verbally, but he often rebels against it. As the later development of this essay will show, he is especially attentive to his bodily experience, a circumstance that will correct the errors of his mind and enable him to exercise freedom without fear. Meanwhile, let us look at an alternative mode of action that he discusses in the remainder of the early text.

In surveying the whole field of the irrational, he has saved for last the phenomena that smack of sorcery (even though some of them are found in the Bible). These have one thing in common: the imagination of one person acts on the bodies of others; like an evil eye, it "launches darts that can injure an external object." Among the various examples given, one catches our attention: "^A Tortoises and ostriches hatch [*couvent*] their eggs just by looking at them, a sign that their sight has some ejaculative virtue" (*DB/I*, p. 71; *OC*, p. 103; *S*, p. 75). We have seen that *la couvade* represents the "feminine" mode of relaxation and productivity toward which Montaigne was moving. We have also seen that when this group of essays was written (about 1572) he was far too tense to "settle" and "brood" over anything. How interesting, therefore, to find him characterizing magic as an attempt to hatch eggs by ejaculative means.

In this concluding section, the power of imagination for productive purposes is confused with use of the imagination for destructive ends; and though attracted by this ambiguous power, Montaigne feels obliged to disclaim the attraction. For right from the first he warns us, "To me, magicians are poor authorities." He does not let this hinder him from repeating stories of apparent sorcery, but he does apologize for their doubtful authenticity. "For I refer the stories that I recite to the consciences of those from whom I have them."

This *caveat*, which closes the first version of the essay, epitomizes Montaigne's plight at age 39. With his new-found leisure, he lives increasingly in imagination; and his lifelong fondness for literature can now be indulged even to excess. The curious stories that come to his attention, and the fantasies they inspire in his mind, have a creative potential in that they demonstrate human freedom, which he may exercise to develop and transform himself. But this freedom is also potentially destructive, both because it can be used for aggression and because it can involve one in falsehood. Since he fears error and aggressiveness, he feels bound to resist speculation and fantasy.[4]

Speculation and fantasy, however, are to him irresistible. In the *B* version (1588), he adds yet another tale of sexual metamorphosis, and speculates further on the operations of tension and desire. Accordingly, he feels obliged to elaborate his apology: "ᴮ The reflections are my own, and depend on the proofs of reason, not of experience; everyone can add his own examples to them; and he who has none, let him not fail

---

[4] If we ask why he should fear aggressiveness and error, we come to the question of social conflict, both external and internalized, which will be discussed in Chapter Five.

to believe that there are plenty, in view of the number and variety of occurrences" (*OC*, p. 104; *S*, p. 75).

This statement misrepresents Montaigne's method and purposes, since by the time he published it he had already written Book Three of the *Essays*, in which reason is everywhere subordinated to experience. But even in the essay on imagination, had he seen clearly, he would have recognized that he had already subordinated judgment and argument to the free association of ideas. How else could he explain his progression from the "imaginary enema" that inspired the essay to disease, death, sexual metamorphosis, impotence, and the evil eye? In fact, the essay itself is an example of imagination circumventing his defenses against it.

In the final version of this essay, much amended, Montaigne takes account of what has happened. Within the first three sentences, he has changed *appréhension* to *imagination* and *transformez* to *renversez*, the last connoting, in addition to lying down, being knocked down and being turned over. Then he adds, "°Its impression on me is piercing" (*OC*, p. 95; *S*, p. 68). His new attitude might be summed up in the proverbial advice: "When rape is inevitable, relax and enjoy it."

His language reflects the change. In contrast to Gallus Vibius, who "bound his soul," Montaigne now speaks of his own "unbound thoughts." Whereas contagion and the evil eye involved "fixing one's gaze," impotence can be cured by a "reverie." His writing no longer serves to resist imagination but only to divert it: "°Et mon art est de luy eschapper, non pas de luy resister."

Relaxation involves being open to risk. "°I catch the disease that I study, and lodge it in me [*le couche en moy*]." Openness requires that one tolerate visions of death and disease, and even perhaps the physical reality. We recall that Montaigne, after years of picturing to himself the frightful ravages of the kidney stone, has at last contracted it. But he has found it bearable and learned that it comes and goes. Likewise, in the matter of impotence, he advises married couples, who have plenty of time, to "take it easy" and wait for the body to reassert itself (*OC*, pp. 99–100; *S*, p. 72). Risks are not defeats.

One can count on organic rhythms, but one can also take the initiative by playing tricks on one's mind. Such, after all, was the strategy of the Toulousain's enema, and such was the method Montaigne himself employed to restore a friend to potency on his wedding night. The tale of his *singeries* on behalf of the Comte de Gurson involves, as he puts it, "a counterbattery of enchantments" used for benevolent ends. He has put into practice what he knew in principle—that sorcery is no more than imagination at work—and the experiment has confirmed his belief. In order to do this he has had to cheat (*contrepipper*), in defiance of his better judgment. "° It was a sudden and curious whim that led me to do such a thing, which was alien to my nature" (*OC*, p. 99; *S*, p. 71). This impulsive and willing inconsistency displays a mental relaxation that parallels his physical relaxation in the face of disease. If the rhythms of the body can teach the mind to relax, then the free play of imagination can restore bodily spontaneity.

It would be pointless to inquire which comes first in these matters, since body and mind are inseparable for Montaigne. Thus his defense of freedom, usually considered an attribute of the soul, is argued entirely by an appeal to the body. He begins by remarking on the independence of the penis, which continually challenges the authority of will. Then, in the style of an attorney in court, he pleads for the exoneration of "monsieur ma partie" on the ground that our whole body is self-regulating and rebellious. Phallic rebellion is ultimately pro-creative, whereas anal rebellion is comical (as witnessed by a collection of stories about farting); but the aggressive element in both must be accepted as a necessary force in life. "° The lawyers and judges quarrel and pass sentence in vain; Nature will meanwhile go her way" (*OC*, p. 101; *S*, p. 73).

Because Nature overrules our will, judgment must relax and imagination have free play. But Montaigne does feel the need to justify this freedom and the literary voyeurism or exhibitionism to which it leads him more than once in this essay. (The rape may be inevitable, but he all too obviously enjoys it.) Hence his role of attorney for the defense and his final appeal to Eros, the Platonic daemon who lifts our generative desire to spiritual heights.

Nowhere better than in the final additions to this essay can we see the parallels between the psychic, social, and historical aspects of Montaigne's literary development. The mock trial in which he asserts his "phallic" independence is simultaneously a rebellion against his mental defenses and a defiance of the social authority represented by the Parlement. It implicates his father, his class, the legalism of the middle ages, the emerging royal and national power, and his long years of involvement with them. Its stylistic extravagance mocks them all, as well as his own earlier seriousness, and it has the exuberance of an impulse long repressed. At the same time, in a long addition at the end of the essay (*OC*, pp. 104–5; *S*, pp. 75–76), he restates his opinion of fantasy and falsehood, and his conclusions reveal a general shift from medieval to modern epistemology.

In medieval thought, truth was accessible to man because the phenomena of this world were God's creations and thus manifestations of ultimate reality. To a skeptic like Montaigne, there is no such easy access to the absolute. Since our senses are unreliable, and our interpretations of phenomena at variance with one another, he has already concluded (in the "Apology for Raymond Sebond") that we have no communication with Being except by the extraordinary intervention of God's grace (*OC*, pp. 586–89; *S*, pp. 455–57). The most certain knowledge attainable, he feels, is a knowledge of his "inner springs." It is the most useful, too, for it allows him to understand the processes by which his opinions are formed, and thus to verify his interpretations of reality.

Psychological knowledge, then, is a safeguard against error in a world where God no longer guarantees the truth. Now Montaigne can justify his use of hearsay evidence:

° So in the study that I am making of our behavior and motives, fabulous testimonies, provided they are possible, serve like true ones. Whether they have happened or no, in Paris or in Rome, to John or Peter, they exemplify, at all events, some human potentiality, and thus their telling imparts useful information to me. I see it and profit from it just as well in shadow as in substance. (*OC,* p. 104; *S,* p. 75.)

His imagination is a trustworthy guide in these matters because the evidence he wants is psychological, and (as Freud also discovered) the "depths" of the mind are often more clearly revealed in fantasy than in reason. If he were to write history, he tells us, he would feel obliged to eschew all speculation and present only verified facts. Indeed, in reporting what he has personally experienced, he is more scrupulous than the Scholastics themselves. But he is temperamentally unsuited to such rigorous work—"ennemy juré d'obligation" —and has undertaken to say only what he knows how to say. Otherwise, he might publish "illegitimate and punishable judgments."

Thus free association, the basis of Montaigne's method— "ma liberté, estant si libre"—is made the virtue of his style. He justifies it obliquely by a reference to Plutarch, whose works may be based on questionable sources, but are unquestionably "useful to posterity, and presented with a luster which lights our way to virtue." In this one assertion of freedom Montaigne abandons law for literature, history for the essay, and judgment for imagination. He recognizes that the value of his work lies not in the certainty of his conclusions but in the novelty of his explorations, and renounces "ulti-mate truth" for self-knowledge.

We have come a long way with Montaigne in this essay. We have seen him apprehensive of imagination because its freedom frightens him. We have seen him intuit its thera-peutic power. We have seen how free association leads him to base mental freedom on the spontaneity of the body, and we have seen the consequences of this approach in his style.[5] Finally, we have seen how the insistent temptations of fantasy, sorcery, and verbal rebellion have forced him to inten-sify his psychological pursuits and to articulate his method and his standards for evidence, which differ fundamentally from those of an earlier age. Thus does an individual, in the course of his personal liberation, contribute to the process of cultural change.

[5] Imbrie Buffum (pp. 26–29) has characterized Montaigne's style as "incar-national," an attempt to embody ideas in fleshly terms.

5. *"Of Custom, and Not Easily Changing an Accepted Law"*

By this time we should accept that Montaigne's roving method of composition usually conceals an essay's underlying structure. In fact, I think we must assume that even where a coherent groundplan is discernible, the author himself could scarcely have told us what it is. Such is the case with the essay on custom (I: 23). It takes more discipline than Montaigne may have possessed to discover that the entire rambling discourse is grounded in a seemingly irreconcilable opposition between individual freedom and political stability.

Like death and imagination, custom (or habit—the French word means both) is pictured in version *A* as a force depriving us of our liberty. It is the assailant from whom Montaigne has fled to his study: "ᴬ But the principal effect of its power is to seize and ensnare us in such a way that it is hardly within our power to get ourselves back out of its grip and return into ourselves to reflect and reason about its ordinances" (*DB*/I, p. 76; *OC*, p. 114; *S*, p. 83). Custom forces the body and impresses the soul, as Montaigne's examples testify. Its authority is established over us without our knowledge or consent in a variety of ways. It is infused in our soul by the seed of our fathers and sucked in with our mothers' milk, he says, acknowledging the extent to which we are determined by our upbringing as well as by our bodily inheritance.

Custom is "a treacherous schoolmistress"—an oblique way of implicating pedagogues in the conspiracy against our freedom. And it is enshrined in the cumbersome system of laws and legal precedents, to which, throughout his thirteen years as a member of the Bordeaux Parlement, Montaigne has had to profess allegiance. Those thirteen years have taught him the difference between laws and justice, between his role as a magistrate and his personal feelings. Now, retired from the Parlement, he is free to attack not only the obscurity and confusion of the laws themselves, but the entire system that treats justice as a commodity for sale, sets up lawyers and magistrates as a fourth estate in opposition to the nobility, and contradicts the rules of honor.

Montaigne is in full rebellion against custom and determined to rid himself of its "violent prejudice" (*DB*/I, p. 77; *OC*, p. 116; *S*, pp. 84–85). The authority of custom hides from us the true face of things, and this mask must be ripped off. It soon appears, however, that this rebellion is all wind. Montaigne has no more intention of defying the laws than of outraging the common style of dress; he will merely retire into himself and pass judgment on them:

ᴬ It seems to me . . . that the wise man should withdraw his soul within, out of the crowd, and keep it in freedom and power to judge things freely; but as for externals, he should wholly follow the accepted fashions and forms. Society in general can do without our thoughts; but the rest—our actions, our work, our fortunes, and our very life—we must lend and abandon to its service and to the common opinions. (*DB*/I, p. 79; *OC*, p. 117; *S*, p. 86.)

If we ask why freedom must be confined to the mind and may not extend to actual reform, his answer is soon forthcoming: because the *state* cannot tolerate change. A government, he says, is like a building so constructed that to shake one part of it is to endanger the whole. And he shores up this position with references to historical advocates of inflexibility.

It is perhaps understandable that even so independent a spirit as Montaigne would take this stand in a time of civil war and personal anxiety. Yet he does realize that it is too rigid, and adds that wisdom teaches us, in cases of extremity, to give way a little rather than risk losing everything (even Sparta furnishes examples of this). So he ends with a compromise: in rare cases, the state may bend slightly to the pressure for change; but the citizen who sees through its falsehood and injustice will nevertheless conform to its laws and keep his opinions to himself. The tension in this position is obvious, and the compromise is unstable and uncomfortable. To a man who loves comfort as Montaigne does, there must be some cure. In fact, the essay itself can be seen as an attempt to relieve the discomfort by objectifying it.

But the problem gets worse before a cure can be found, and in the *B* version of 1588 the opposing positions are intensified. Examples of strange customs collected from Montaigne's reading are multiplied in an extraordinary passage beginning "Il est des peuples où . . ." and repeating the "où" in each of 32 consecutive sentences that describe exotic sexual and funerary rites, mutilation, cannibalism, idolatry, and incest. "ᴮ Where the fathers lend their children, the husbands their wives, to their guests to enjoy, for money. Where a man can respectably have children by his mother, and fathers have sexual relations with their daughters, and with their sons" (*OC*, pp. 112–13; *S*, p. 82).

Each repetition of the syllable *où* snaps another link in the chain of social restraint, and we drift farther and farther from our customary moorings. Montaigne seems almost to be carried away on the waves of licentious images. At the same time, the customs are described with a precision that betrays detachment, or even irony, and the whole reverie is used to demonstrate that somewhere in the world every "wild fantasy" of which humans are capable has been justified by reason. In other words, there can be no universally dependable criterion for condemning incest or any other "forbidden" behavior. Like the houses in one of those far-off lands, "où tout est ouvert," the doors of Montaigne's mind are wide open; and his only security is in clinging to the customs and laws of his own culture simply because they are customary.

It is not surprising that Montaigne, having glimpsed the implications of cultural relativism, is anxious to defend his country against religious and political reform. Once begun, how can it reasonably be contained? Hence the intolerant tone of his *B* additions to the second half of the essay, where his concern is no longer with personal freedom but with national stability:

> B I am disgusted with innovation, in whatever guise, and with reason, for I have seen very harmful effects of it. . . . Those who give the first shock to a state are apt to be the first ones swallowed up in its ruin. The unity and contexture of this monarchy, this great structure, having been dislocated and dissolved, especially in its old age, by this innovation, as wide an entry as one could wish is opened to similar attacks. (*OC*, p. 118; *S*, pp. 86–87.)

His images tell the story: to sway the state (*donner le branle*) is to open it to ruin (*donner . . . d'ouverture et d'entrée*). It is a problem of dynamics, of movement and obstruction; and once again Montaigne, for whom soul and body are inseparable, chooses the metaphor of anal retention to express the situation. Speaking of reformers, he says:

> B Their medicine has the same effect as other medicines that are weak and ill applied: the humors that it wanted to purge in us it has heated, exasperated, and embittered by the conflict, and still it has remained in our body. It has not been able to purge us because of its weakness, and yet it has weakened us so that we cannot evacuate it either; and all we get from its operation is long intesti-

nal pains. . . . The ordinary discipline of a state that is in a healthy condition does not provide for these extraordinary accidents; it presupposes a body that holds together in its principal parts and functions, and a common consent to its observance and obedience. (*OC*, p. 121; *S*, p. 89.)

"A body that holds together" is one in which retention and elimination alternate in an overall pattern that is stable and healthy. In the sick state of France, by contrast, obstruction and purgation work stubbornly against each other.

In the previous chapter, we saw how Montaigne came to recognize "the fact that experience is anchored in the ground plan of the body."[1] Now we see an extension of "organ modes" into yet another dimension: not only personal behavior but also the conduct of the state is to be interpreted in bodily terms. This metaphor may seem merely an application of the Renaissance commonplace that state and individual are related as macrocosm to microcosm. But the broader analogy itself is an acknowledgment that human institutions function like the beings who form them. This is the full meaning of the phrase, "the body politic."[2]

Montaigne's interpretation of the state of France at this time conforms to his own mental state, as the essay reveals. His "anal crisis" is unresolved; and while his imagination runs to licentious extremes, he resists political transformations. Afraid of the consequences of inner freedom, he advocates keeping one's thoughts held in. Not until the final version of the text is this opposition absorbed into a larger pattern of mutuality and moderation.

Emblematic of the change is the story he tells in version *C* about father-beating:

ᶜThe man whom they found beating his father replied that it was the custom of his house: that his father had beaten his grand-

---

[1] Erikson, *Childhood and Society*, p. 108.
[2] See Brown, Chapter I.

father thus, his grandfather his great-grandfather; and, pointing to his son: "And this one will beat me when he has come to my present age." And the father whom his son was dragging and bumping along the street ordered him to stop at a certain door, for he had dragged his own father only that far; this was the limit of the hereditary rough treatment that the sons traditionally practiced upon the fathers in their family. (*OC*, pp. 113–14; *S*, p. 83.)

If he formerly felt rebellious, he now feels that he has gone far enough, even though opposition to the old ways is a necessary stage of development.[3]

He does not repudiate his critique of custom. On the contrary, he carries it further, applying it as much to French mores as to those of primitive societies. He recognizes that "natural" and "unnatural" love, the laws of conscience, and even the distinction between sanity and madness are all defined by social convention:

° The laws of conscience, which we say are born of nature, are born of custom. Each man, holding in inward veneration the opinions and the behavior approved and accepted around him, cannot break loose from them without remorse, or apply himself to them without self-satisfaction. (*OC*, p. 114; *S*, p. 83.)

° Whence it comes to pass that what is off the hinges of custom, people believe to be off the hinges of reason: God knows how unreasonably, most of the time. (*Ibid.*)

° In truth, chastity is a fine virtue, whose utility is well enough known; but to treat it and justify it according to nature is as hard as it is easy to justify it according to custom, laws, and precepts. (*OC*, p. 115; *S*, p. 84.)

If so much may be granted to be arbitrary, why not admit that forms of government, on occasion, may also be changed with profit? First, Montaigne describes a nation "where they

---

[3] For an explicit statement on the necessity of opposing one's elders, see I: 22, "One Man's Profit Is Another Man's Harm."

vary the form of government according as affairs require" (*OC*, p. 112; *S*, p. 81), and then he makes fun of a custom-ridden people who, having rid themselves of an oppressive monarch, hasten to replace him with another (*OC*, pp. 114–15; *S*, pp. 83–84). This turning of the weapons of relativism upon one's own defenses he presents as a bold new strategy, developed through self-study. Formerly, we may assume, he was like those teachers who, finding "first and universal reasons hard to scrutinize," fall back on custom to justify their precepts (*OC*, pp. 115–16; *S*, p. 84). Now he admits that custom can justify him no more than the next man. This has consequences for both himself and others:

° If, as we who study ourselves have learned to do, each man who hears a true statement immediately considered how it properly pertains to him, each man would find that it is not so much a good saying as a good whiplash to the ordinary stupidity of his judgment. But men receive the advice of truth and its precepts as if addressed to the common people, never to themselves; and each man, instead of incorporating them into his behavior, incorporates them into his memory, very stupidly and uselessly. (*OC*, p. 114; *S*, p. 83.)

Although this "good whiplash" strikes Montaigne's own judgment sharply, it must cut even more deeply into those who have not learned to study themselves. Such, for instance, are the Catholic extremists, against whom Montaigne now speaks out boldly, accusing them of using unmistakable vices to combat debatable errors (*OC*, p. 119; *S*, p. 87). His "moderation" is not a colorless abstention from judgment but a vigorous mixture of self-limitation and censure of the presumptuous. Retention and aggression serve in turn.

Although first expressed here, this attitude is not really new to Montaigne, who tells us that he has been a foe to presumption since his youth. What is new is the courage with which he now states his moderate position. "° Private reason has only a private jurisdiction" (*OC*, p. 120; *S*, p. 88). So much is true. But (belatedly, we might say) he has discovered that private reason can be a public force by virtue of its publication. By exhibiting the fruits of his self-study to the world, he has put his independence at the service of the state. His essays provide a middle term between individual freedom and political stability.

As we might expect, the essay form has developed greater flexibility while effecting this moral synthesis. Rebelliousness, obstinacy, and fear now alternate with expressions of moderation, irony, and courage. Montaigne now interrupts a passage on the ill effects of habit to make the contrary point that his own meticulous honesty results from early habituation (*OC*, p. 108; *S*, p. 79). In the midst of his long list of foreign customs, he ostentatiously digresses: "° Let us here steal room for a story" (*OC*, p. 109; *S*, p. 80). And so on to the end. The whole essay, which once concerned the dangers of instability, has now become a *branle*—one of Montaigne's favorite words, which can depict the tottering of a state, the swing of a pendulum, or the patterned movement of a dance.

The relation between Montaigne and his public begins to appear here—and, of course, to affect his relations with himself. In the next few chapters we will consider a group of essays begun between 1578 and 1580, when the prospect of publication began to influence all his work.

6. *"Of Giving the Lie"*

In the preceding chapter, we observed a slow dialectic whereby private thoughts and public action were synthesized in the process of publication: that is, warring tendencies toward retention and aggression, symptomatic of anxiety, were mediated by Montaigne's development as a writer, and, integrated in a courageous and flexible personality, became mutually reinforcing tendencies toward self-limitation and self-assertion. This same dialectical movement is apparent in the next essay to be dealt with (II: 18), but the terms are somewhat different. Here we are dealing with false modesty and lying, which are also transformed through the medium of print.

This short essay, "Of Giving the Lie," seems at first glance to consist of two sections that have almost nothing to do with each other. In the 1580 text, Montaigne spends two pages defending himself against the charge that only great men should presume to write about their lives and the remaining three pages inveighing against the untruthfulness of his age and nation. The two themes are linked by only the weakest of rhetorical questions: "ᴬ But, to tell the truth, whom shall we believe when he talks about himself, in so corrupt an age, seeing that there are few or none whom we can believe when they speak of others, where there is less incentive for lying?" (*DB*/II, p. 243; *OC*, p. 649; *S*, p. 505).

A careful rereading of the essay, however, may show us a much stronger connection between these two themes than the author himself could articulate, and that is the fact that in his first two pages Montaigne himself has not been entirely truthful.

> ▲ I am not building here a statue to erect at the town crossroads, or in a church or a public square: this is to hide in the nook of a library, and to amuse someone who has a particular interest in knowing me: a neighbor, a relative, a friend who may take pleasure in associating and conversing with me again in this image. Others have taken courage to speak of themselves because they found the subject worthy and rich; I, on the contrary, because I have found mine so barren and so meager that no suspicion of ostentation can fall upon my plan. . . . All the contact that I have with the public in this is that I have been obliged to borrow their tools of printing, as being swifter and easier: I have had to cast this image in a mold in order to avoid the trouble of having several copies of it made by hand. (*DB*/II, pp. 242–43; *OC*, pp. 646–47; *S*, p. 503.)

We may not want to accuse Montaigne of an outright lie at this point, for he has not yet published any of his essays and does not know how wide a public they will attract. Yet he intends to publish them, since he talks of having them cast in print. It may indeed have seemed to him that he was "borrowing" the tools of printing for the sake of convenience alone, but this illusion can only be secured by a sustained inattention to the facts of the matter. He either does not realize or will not admit that "a library" in his case really means "several hundred or several thousand libraries." Immediately before the passage we have quoted, he compares himself to Horace, who recited only to friends and in private; but he refuses to admit that whereas Horace had to recite orally from manuscript or memory, the printed essays will be available to a large and not necessarily select public.

Montaigne's inability to acknowledge this new situation may be motivated by anxiety about the change. By casting his "private" thoughts in a new medium, he is being both innovative and presumptuous, regardless of his disclaimers. Hence it is not surprising to see him, in one of his few additions of 1588, suggesting that lying betrays a lack of courage (*OC*, p. 649; *S*, p. 505). In this essay, as in so many others, it is not until version *C* that he declares the truth. It is an exemplary case of form following function: exactly at the breach between the halves of his essay, he inserts a long passage on his medium—which mediates between the halves. He no longer pretends to write for friends and family alone, but admits that his moral observations are often intended for the public:

ᶜ How many times, irritated by some action that civility and reason kept me from reproving openly, have I disgorged it here, not without ideas of instructing the public! And indeed, these poetic lashes—

> Bang in the eye, bang on the snout,
> Bang on the back of the apish lout!

—imprint themselves even better on paper than on living flesh. (*OC*, p. 648; *S*, pp. 504-5.)

This modification of the position expressed in the first half of the essay provides the latter half with its *raison d'être*: his artful reflections on lying and its effects are designed to instruct his countrymen at large. No ancient satirist, we must remember, could have hoped for the readership that the printing press will give Montaigne.[1] Only now does he seem fully aware of this fact.

---

[1] For a useful discussion of the ancient custom of reading aloud, and of the altered relationship between author and public after the advent of printing, see McLuhan, pp. 84-85, 130-33.

He is aware of other things as well. Having formerly spoken of casting his image in the printer's mold, he now develops the metaphor into something far more complex and revealing:

° In modeling this figure upon myself, I have had to fashion and compose myself so often to bring myself out, that the model itself has to some extent grown firm and taken shape. Painting myself for others, I have painted my inward self with colors clearer than my original ones. I have no more made my book than my book has made me—a book consubstantial with its author, concerned with my own self, an integral part of my life; not concerned with some third-hand, extraneous purpose, like all other books. (*OC*, pp. 647–48; *S*, p. 504.)

This passage has often been noted, and I need not give it still another exegesis. But I would like to point out one of its implications: that the "myself" on which Montaigne's book is modeled is, like the book itself, a *construct* created by his ego. He does not possess an absolute and unalterable Self; rather, he paints, and can repaint, his Self in his mind (*en moy*). Only thus is it possible for his book to have made him as much as he has made it. When he says, then, that the book is an integral part of his life, we must take him seriously. In the book his existence is mediated by printed words; in his Self it is no less mediated by thought.[2] In both cases, the media are, in McLuhan's phrase, extensions of the man. Having

---

[2] "Self-knowledge, like any art or science, renders its subject-matter in a new medium, the medium of ideas, in which it loses its old dimensions and its old place." Santayana, p. 134. The distinction implied by Santayana, between self-knowledge and its subject-matter, I would translate into a distinction between one's Self and one's individuality. The latter is much closer to the popular conception of one's innermost being; but it is an unconscious attribute of the ego process, a mere continuity and consistency of bodily and mental activity. In order to become conscious, individuality must be objectified and mediated by thought (involving memory, imagination, and language), and thus it becomes Self.

externalized his subject/object dichotomy in the form of a book, he is now literally a tripartite creature.

Without anticipating the conclusions of the remaining chapters, let us enumerate some of the effects of this evolution in selfhood. First, in guiding his behavior Montaigne now has two models to which he can refer: a Self and a self-image. One is intrapsychic and relatively fluid, the other external and fixed in print. Second, a continual interplay between ego, Self, and literary self-image renders Montaigne more intensely but also more effectively self-conscious, since he is in a better position to use his self-knowledge for self-criticism, self-control, and further self-construction. The inner split has given him power over himself. Finally, the inner division is accompanied by what we might call an outer integration: he is simultaneously (rather than alternately) public and private. Indeed, nothing is more public about him than his most solitary cogitations in his book-lined tower.

Each of these changes has been effected by the process of self-externalization. What is particularly interesting in this essay is that Montaigne's reflections on the process itself, as expressed in the long central interpolation, transform bad faith to good. In the early version, he indulges in false modesty, trying to pass off a sermon on lying as a memento for his grandchildren. But in its final state, the essay achieves a truthful estimate of both his self-portrayal and his moral instruction. In fact, the two are now inseparable: he *teaches* by grasping and writing down what he *is*.

° Have I wasted my time by taking stock of myself so continually, so carefully? For those who go over themselves only in their minds and occasionally in speech do not penetrate to essentials in their examination as does a man who makes that his study, his work, and his trade, who binds himself to keep an enduring account, with all his faith, with all his strength. (*OC*, p. 648; *S*, p. 504.)

By articulating his own divided nature, Montaigne has overcome the duplicity in his public posture and also repaired the split in the structure of his essay. Implicit in this movement from pretense to honesty is the relationship between style and truth, and this is the problem Montaigne confronts in the next essay I shall discuss.

7. *"Of the Education of Children"*

The false modesty in which Montaigne indulged while writing "Of Giving the Lie" becomes an elaborately developed pose in the opening pages of his essay on the education of children (I: 26, version *A*). He manages, amid protestations of ignorance and incompetence, to let us know that he has been urged by someone who read his essay on pedantry to write more on the subject of education; that he believes this to be the most difficult and important problem confronting human knowledge; and that being on the best of terms with a distinguished lady whose family is noted for its learning, he is going to offer her a bit of unconventional advice on how to educate her yet unborn son.

Although he presents it as "a single, fanciful idea," Montaigne's advice comprehends an entire theory of education, spread out over 25 pages (by far the longest essay in Book One). In the concluding section, while reiterating the inadequacies of his own formal education and portraying himself as a lazy and almost totally indifferent student, he nevertheless demonstrates that he is preeminently qualified to give advice to others. In fact, he is a living example of the type of education he advocates, having eschewed traditional book-learning in favor of wisdom, independence, and integrity. We should not overlook, among his numerous self-deprecations, such sentences as these:

ᴬ What I saw, I saw with a certain and open-minded judgment, and beneath this inert appearance nourished bold ideas and opinions beyond my years. (*DB*/I, p. 127; *OC*, p. 174; *S*, p. 129.)

ᴬ Meanwhile, my mind was not lacking in strong stirrings of its own, which it digested alone and without communication. And, among other things, I really do believe that it would have been wholly incapable of submitting to force and violence. (*DB*/I, p. 129; *OC*, p. 176; *S*, p. 131.)

He begins by insisting that learning, as represented by the professional scholar, is beyond him: "Ce n'est pas mon occupation" (*DB*/I, p. 101). But he ends by demonstrating that he is no mere professional, but something definitely superior: a gentleman who is well-rounded (as we say) in practical accomplishments, both moral and physical.

The affectation of modesty in this essay and elsewhere has little to do with Montaigne's actual opinion of himself. It is, in fact, a literary convention established by ancient and medieval writers on the theory that a show of humility will render the reader more receptive to their opinions.[1] In practice, of course, the convention often calls attention less to the author's humility than to his worth. But if the device is deliberately used for this purpose, it must be handled with delicacy—that is, made almost believable and kept inconspicuous. That the persistent self-contradiction in this essay is less apparent than I have made it seem is due to Montaigne's agility and the gracefulness of his courtly manners; his hopping from one attitude to another, if we notice it at all, seems like an amusing and ingratiating dance.

[1] See the discussion of the modesty *topos* in Curtius, pp. 83–85.

Such elegance and skill, however, involve yet another contradiction, for they are quite out of keeping with what Montaigne says about his style. In the first place, although quoting a good deal from ancient sources, he feels obliged to say that this is a foolish practice, since it only shows up the poverty of his writing by comparison with theirs. If he were to patch up his ill-formed arguments with those of Plutarch, he maintains, the result would be a monstrosity, so far is he beneath his idol. In fact, he persistently underrates his own originality and finesse. When he claims to leave his "ineptitudes" unretouched so as to furnish us with a more candid self-portrait, the disparity between his exaggerated modesty and his pretended frankness is all the more striking:

ᴬ However that may be, I mean to say, and whatever these absurdities may be, I have had no intention of concealing them, any more than I would a bald and graying portrait of myself, in which the painter had drawn not a perfect face, but mine. For likewise these are my humors and opinions; I offer them as what I believe, not what is to be believed. I aim here only at revealing myself, who will perhaps be different tomorrow, if I learn something new which changes me. I have no authority to be believed, nor do I want it, feeling myself too ill-instructed to instruct others. (*DB*/I, p. 103; *OC*, p. 147; *S*, pp. 108–9.)

But we have already seen that his self-presentation is intended to instruct the public; indeed, the motive force of his style is precisely the "desire to be believed."

Later, he returns to the subject of style, and declares himself the enemy of affectation, as if his arch humility were unaffected:

ᴬ The speech I love is a simple, natural [*naïf*] speech, the same on paper as in the mouth; a speech succulent and sinewy, brief and compressed, rather difficult than boring, remote from affectation and artifice, irregular, disconnected, and bold; each bit making a body in itself; not pedantic, not monkish, not lawyer-like, but rather soldierly, as Suetonius calls Julius Caesar's speech. (*DB*/I, pp. 123–24; *OC*, p. 171; *S*, p. 127.)

An admirable definition, we might agree, and beautifully expressed. But what simple, naïve soldier could have written it? The fact is that Montaigne is attempting in this first version of the essay to *sound* simple and naïve while advocating some of the most sophisticated ideas of his age. Moreover, he assumes the same kind of sophistication in his audience, that small group of aristocrats to whom learning is a suitable ornament (see *DB*/I, p. 104). His "fantasy" is intended to impress the reader as a careless masterpiece—as a stylistic *tour de force* requiring but concealing the greatest effort and skill.

Now, in a truly naïve writer this contradiction might be attributed to bad faith, to a real lack of awareness of what he was doing and how well he was doing it. But in Montaigne's case, it appears to be deliberate craft of the sort recommended by Castiglione in *The Book of the Courtier*: that is, *sprezzatura*, an aristocratic nonchalance that conceals all art.² What is striking about the later versions of this essay is that even as Montaigne greatly elaborates his artfulness, he simultaneously gives away the show.

The very first *B* addition to the text concerns the theme of self-concealment:

ᴮ Look at Cimon, look at Themistocles and a thousand others, how they belied themselves. The young of bears and dogs show their natural inclination, but men, plunging headlong into certain habits, opinions, and laws, easily change or disguise themselves. (*OC*, p. 148; *S*, p. 109.)

---

² Castiglione, pp. 40–45. Villey (I, 102) thinks it likely that Montaigne had been familiar with a French translation of Castiglione in his youth; and we definitely know that he reread the book after 1588. In any case, the principle of *sprezzatura* was one that Montaigne could have absorbed from any number of the ancient works in his library. For a fuller treatment of this subject, see Lapp, *The Esthetics of Negligence*.

The essay on custom has shown us how much Montaigne felt his own inclinations had been buried under "habits, opinions, and laws." And a major task of his middle years is a self-searching that brings to light traits that have been buried within him by enculturation. In the additions to I: 26 we shall see him publish two related discoveries: first, that in submitting to the convention of modesty he has been untrue to his natural bent for self-revelation; second, that his literary style is built on the foundations of his social behavior. It is simply an extension of gentlemanly conduct.

Many of the interpolations of 1588 are merely quotations and paraphrases, and I shall have something to say about them later. Just now we should look at two longer additions that link Montaigne's style of writing with his style of behavior. To the passage in which he praises "soldierly" simplicity and unaffectedness, he adds the following:

> ᴮ I have been prone to imitate that disorder in dress which we see in our young men—a cloak worn like a scarf, the hood over one shoulder, a neglected stocking—which shows a pride disdainful of these foreign adornments and careless of art. But I think it is even better employed in our form of speech. (*OC*, p. 171; *S*, p. 127.)

Between the naïveté of a soldier and the disdainful pride of a student there is a very great difference. Furthermore, Montaigne admits that in his case the "disorder" is an imitation, making it doubly self-conscious.

The most telling change, however, comes at the end of the essay, where Montaigne suddenly seems to remember an experience that might be relevant to his youthful self-confidence:

> ᴮ Shall I include in my account this faculty of my boyhood, assurance in expression and flexibility in voice and gesture, in adapting myself to the parts I undertook to act? For before the usual age,
>
> > Scarce had my twelfth year snatched me
> > > from the year before,

I played the leading parts in the Latin tragedies of Buchanan, Guerente, and Muret, which were performed with dignity in our Collège de Guyenne. In this matter, as in all other parts of his job, Andreas Goveanus, our principal, was incomparably the greatest principal of France; and I was considered a master craftsman. Acting is an exercise that I do not at all disapprove of for young children of good family; and since then I have seen our princes take part in it in person, honorably and commendably, after the example of some of the ancients. (*OC*, p. 176; *S*, p. 131.)

Here we have the deliberate nonchalance of which he had spoken earlier ("Shall I include in my account?"), as well as a frank admission of his skill as a performer. Here also we have a clue to why the problem of literary style has occupied him to such an extent in an essay on education. Montaigne is becoming conscious of the fact (though he does not yet state it explicitly) that education is a kind of dramatic training. His essay prescribes how boys can best be prepared to play a *role*, that of "gentleman." But note that in writing it, he is also demonstrating how the role should be played. "Young children of good family" (that is, the sons of the nobility), and even princes, must do in life what he does in his book: they must cultivate style.

To a man who is determined to portray his true self, the discovery that he has been playing a role must be disconcerting. Yet Montaigne cannot permanently ignore the evidence of his own stylistic achievements. If only to justify his book, he is obliged to work out the relation between style and truth. By advocating nonchalance in speech as in dress, he has already revealed an awareness of how much art there is in life. Extending the same passage in version *C*, he further blurs the distinction between the two:

° Any affectation, especially in the gaiety and freedom of French, is unbecoming to a courtier. And in a monarchy every gentleman should be trained in the manner of a courtier. Wherefore we do

well to lean a little in the direction of naturalness and negligence.
(*OC*, p. 171; *S*, p. 127.)

Earlier in the essay he has spoken of courtly language as untrustworthy, since a courtier must necessarily flatter and deceive (*OC*, p. 154; *S*, p. 114). But here he acknowledges that training is required as much to avoid affectation as to make use of it. The writer, too, must "lean a little in the direction of naturalness" and avoid expressions that call attention to themselves. "Would that I might use only those that are used in the markets of Paris!" exclaims Montaigne. What distinguishes Montaigne and his ideal pupil from the courtier is that their art is employed to reveal rather than conceal the truth.

In his efforts to better express the truth, Montaigne does not shun either careful revisions or stylistic flourishes. A comparison of the first and final texts will reveal, for instance, how much he reworks the remarks on his youthful independence of mind that I have quoted. A glance at the additions labeled *C* will show how many are authoritative, even sententious, in tone. For example: "° He who follows another follows nothing. He finds nothing; indeed he seeks nothing. . . . Let him know that he knows, at least" (*OC*, p. 150; *S*, p. 111). Montaigne's self-confidence is now outspoken.

Yet another way to express the truth about himself, he discovers, is to make capital of his own defects. Deleting the sentence in which he has said that by mixing Plutarch's style with his own he would "engender monsters," he inserts another: "° One needs very strong loins [*reins*—literally, kidneys] to undertake to march abreast of those men" (*OC*, p. 145; *S*, p. 107). We know by now that Montaigne's kidneys were his weakest spot; but it is also obvious that in choosing such a concrete, idiosyncratic, and even intimate image to express his inferiority, he is not walking abreast of Plutarch but has actually surpassed him. He confesses his moral defects as well, confident that the admission is a sign of strength. Always willing to call himself lazy and disorganized, he now adds what his critics say of him: "° Idle; cool in the duties of friendship and kinship, and in public duties; too self-centered" (*OC*, p. 175; *S*, p. 130).

The principle that holds together the increasingly diverse topics and excursions of this essay is one that we have already approached from several angles: Montaigne's own life, the advice he is giving, and the way he gives it are parallel; social behavior, educational theory, and literary style are congruent. In earlier versions of the essay certain discrepancies between these aspects gave evidence of deception, but by their later adjustment to each other they achieve a greater truthfulness.

Before we look further into the quality of this truthfulness, we should consider another aspect of the parallelism. In his advice on education, Montaigne repeatedly states that a young gentleman should not depend excessively on books. Rather, he should appropriate their ideas and use only these to form himself. He should never memorize: "° To know by heart is not to know; it is to retain what we have given our memory to keep. . . . Sad competence, a purely bookish competence!" And of course, for this kind of training the whole world is our book: "ᴬ Now, for this apprenticeship, everything that comes to our eyes is book enough: a page's prank, a servant's blunder, a remark at table, are so many new materials" (*OC*, pp. 151–52; *S*, p. 112).

As if to reflect this situation, Montaigne's book has been expanding to include the whole world. There is almost nothing one cannot find mentioned, particularly in the vast, rambling essays of Book Three. Crammed into it, too, are bits of all the books he has read. But true to his advice, he has not memorized them; he has instead relegated them to his book, where he can forget them and free his mind for the real business of education, which is understanding. "° I have not had regular dealings with any solid book, except Plutarch and Seneca, from whom I draw like the Danaïds, incessantly filling up and pouring out. Some of this sticks to this paper; to myself, little or nothing" (*OC*, p. 144; *S*, p. 107).

This is the first time he has been able to find a rationale for the "stuffing" of his essays, a practice that has embarrassed him for years. He can justify it now because he understands the complex relations between himself and his book. The book is a part of him, but a relatively static reflection of the more active, volatile part. It is admirably suited to function as a repository of information from the past, allowing the rest of him to become even more changeable. But if it is accurately to reflect his changeability, he must constantly refashion it. It must exhibit a true image of him as a craftsman; it must even, on occasion, be able to catch him in the act of being crafty. So ambiguous is Montaigne's "truth."

Thus it is that early in version *C* he flatly contradicts his previous statements about rivaling the ancients: "° Still, I well know how audaciously I always attempt to match the level of my pilferings, to keep pace with them, not without a rash hope that I may deceive the eyes of the judges who try to discover them" (*OC*, p. 146; *S*, p. 108). Fourteen pages later, thanks to his painstaking editors, we discover him translating Seneca without acknowledging the source, and then paraphrasing another Senecan sentiment with an unwonted extravagance of poetic language (see *OC*, pp. 160n, 161n; *S*, p. 119). This is no longer a confession of ineptitude but a demonstration of skill.

The open practice of deception has its paradigm in the performance of an actor on a stage, and Montaigne's self-advertised "piperie" is an extension of the talent for playing roles on which he has already congratulated himself. By an ever more penetrating look at what he is doing in the essays, he has been forced to admit that his "self" is to a large extent a performance. And his medium, in order to transmit *that* aspect of his self, must reveal not the role that is played but the actor in the process of performing.

"True" self-knowledge is a "transparent" vision of all aspects of the self.[3] To render this knowledge truthfully, the medium must also be transparent. When it clouds over, as it sometimes does even in Montaigne's later writings, it betrays a momentary fragmentation of his vision, a narrowing of concern accompanied by signs of anxiety. Such is the case, I think, at the point where, having stated the accusations of self-centeredness and lack of charity that his critics have leveled against him, he defends himself in a passage that becomes noticeably tortuous and constricted:

°I should take it as a favor that men should find me wanting only in such acts of supererogation. But they are unjust to demand what I do not owe, much more rigorously than they demand of themselves what they do owe. By condemning me to an action they wipe out all the gratification of it and the gratitude that would be due me for it; whereas the good that I do should have greater weight coming from me, considering that I have none at all done me. (*OC*, p. 176; *S*, p. 130.)[4]

[3] See Heidegger, pp. 186–87. "The sight which is related primarily and on the whole to existence we call *'transparency'* [*Durchsichtigkeit*]. We choose this term to designate 'knowledge of the Self' in a sense which is well understood, so as to indicate that here it is not a matter of perpetually tracking down and inspecting a point called the 'Self,' but rather one of seizing upon the full disclosedness of Being-in-the-world *throughout all* the constitutive items which are essential to it, and doing so with understanding. In existing, entities sight 'themselves' [*sichtet 'sich'*] only in so far as they have become transparent to themselves with equal primordiality in those items which are constitutive for their existence: their Being-alongside the world and their Being-with Others."

[4] The translation is perhaps clearer than the original: "Je recevroy à faveur qu'on ne desirast en moy que tels effects de supererogation. Mais ils sont injustes d'exiger ce que je ne doy pas, plus rigoureusement beaucoup qu'ils n'exigent d'eux ce qu'ils doivent. En m'y condemnant, ils effacent la gratification de l'action et la gratitude qui m'en seroit deuë; là où le bien faire actif devroit plus peser de ma main, en consideration de ce que je n'en ay passif nul qui soit."

This is one of the rare passages in Montaigne so unclear as to have prompted rival interpretations from a number of critics (see *OC*, p. 176n). I doubt that he really intends to show us here just how bothered he is by those who put a finger on the weakest point of his personality, for there is a tension in the syntax that indicates he was probably trying to hide from his own guilt. But such is the flexibility of his style that it calls to our attention those aspects of his existence that he himself may have found opaque.

8. *"Of the Affection of Fathers for Their Children"*

The more accomplished an essayist Montaigne becomes, the harder it is to determine just what he is about. This essay (II: 8) is a case in point. It consists of an elaborate dedication to Mme d'Estissac, a longish discussion of paternal affection, and a concluding reflection on man's works as the children of his soul. For once, the title of the essay does furnish a nominal link between all of its parts, but the functional relationship of those parts is nonetheless puzzling. Why is an essay on fathers and sons dedicated to an especially admirable mother? And why, after lengthy advice to parents on how to manage their family finances so as to be fair to their sons, does Montaigne drift off into musings on ancient history, philosophy, and art, never returning to the concrete situations that concerned him at the start?

In the light of what we have observed in earlier chapters, some elements of this essay stand out: there is the by-now familiar combination of false modesty and confident self-presentation; there is a simultaneous concern with instructing the public, maintaining social position, and indulging private imagination; and there is a recognition of how essential Montaigne's book has become to both his social identity and his emotional balance.

But the essay also contains something that we have not yet encountered, which provides a clue to the unity of Montaigne's discussion. This is the depth of feeling evoked in Montaigne, and reawakened in us, by the story of a father who hid his love for his son:

ᴬ After the late Marshal de Monluc lost his son—in truth a brave gentleman and one of great promise, who died on the island of Madeira—he used to stress greatly to me, among his other regrets, the sorrow and heartbreak he felt for never having opened up to him. He had lost, he said, by that habit of paternal gravity and stiffness, the comfort of appreciating his son and knowing him well, and also of declaring to him the extreme affection that he bore him and the high opinion he had of his virtue. "And that poor boy," he would say, "saw nothing of me but a scowling and disdainful countenance, and took with him the belief that I knew neither how to love him nor how to esteem him according to his merit. For whom was I keeping the revelation of that singular affection that I bore him in my soul? Wasn't he the one who should have had all the pleasure of it and all the gratitude? I constrained and tortured myself to maintain this vain mask, and thereby lost the pleasure of association with him, and of his good will along with it, for he could not be other than very cool toward me, having never had anything but harshness from me or experienced any but a tyrannical bearing." I think this lament was well taken and reasonable; for, as I know by too certain experience, there is no consolation so sweet in the loss of our friends as that which comes to us from the knowledge of not having forgotten to tell them anything and of having had perfect and entire communication with them. (*DB*/I, pp. 327–28; *OC*, pp. 375–76; *S*, p. 287.)

The perfect communication to which Montaigne refers is, of course, his friendship with La Boétie, which he has glowingly described in "Of Friendship." Most likely, Monluc's situation calls to mind an experience of friendship rather than one of paternal affection because Montaigne has no sons. If he had any, he has told us just before presenting this story, he would not shrink from familiarity with them: "ᴬ Even if I could make myself feared, I would much rather make myself loved" (*DB/*I, p. 327; *OC*, p. 373; *S*, p. 285).

"Me faire aymer." The desire to *make himself loved* is the mainspring of Montaigne's literary activity, as I hope to show. This is why he sympathizes with Monluc's complaint. The essay is a response to his own most fundamental need, the working out of a project that we may properly call erotic.

In order to understand the dominance of Montaigne's erotic project, we must briefly review his early experience. The picture he gives us of his childhood is one of the most idyllic in all of literature. Awakened daily by music, he was seduced into an easy familiarity with the classics by indulgent masters, under the benign supervision of a father who had the highest hopes for him. In his first six years he "felt the rod only twice, and that very softly." So artificial and protected was his realm that all who would play an effective role in it had to learn Latin first. There is no indication that he tyrannized his entourage, as such a "model" child might easily have done, but he must have felt himself very much the focus of all eyes and the lodestone of all affections. At the age of six, he was sent to school in Bordeaux. Even there he received preferential treatment at his father's behest, "but for all that, it was still school." He leaves no doubt that he disliked it, and he could hardly have helped feeling that he had been cast out of Paradise.

From childhood until the death of his father, Montaigne seems to have done his best to earn the affection that had at first been given so freely and then, at least to the child's eyes, withdrawn so abruptly. He followed his father into public service, translated Sebond at his father's suggestion, and married the daughter of a parliamentary president in order to fulfill his family obligations. There is no hint that he ever rebelled against the role prepared for him, although there are plenty of indications that he played it without enthusiasm, being from the first a lazy student, a skeptical magistrate, and an indifferent husband. His conformity can best be explained, it seems to me, by a desire to recapture his father's love. The one thing in which he invested himself heavily was his infatuation with La Boétie; and as we read how the two men became so absorbed in each other that the rest of the world was shut out, we can see in that relationship an attempt to regain the exclusive world in which the young Michel's self had existed briefly as a reflection in his father's eyes.

But La Boétie died when Michel was thirty, and Pierre de Montaigne died five years later, each death repeating the childhood crisis. The parliamentary career had proved an inauthentic vocation, and was resigned with audible relief. Translating Sebond, too, must have inspired him with mixed feelings, if the equivocal stance of his later "Apology" for that author is a safe indication of how he felt a decade earlier. And there are frequent hints throughout the essays that his marriage, though tolerable and even comfortable, was neither passionate nor intellectually stimulating.

This last point relates to an important determinant of Montaigne's life: his prejudices regarding women. Many (not to say most) men can recapture the remembered bliss of childhood intimacy more or less successfully through the love of a mistress, a wife, or a daughter. Not so with Montaigne. Early in this essay he stresses his preference for a "truly paternal" affection, based on a rational appreciation by the father of the development of reason in his son, over the "instinctual" love felt by mothers for their infants. "ᴬ Reason alone must guide our inclinations" (*DB*/I, p. 319; *OC*, p. 366; *S*, p. 279).

Near the end of the essay Montaigne again stresses the unreasonableness of women: "ᴬ For that disordered appetite and sick taste that they have at the time of their pregnancies they have in their soul at all times" (*DB*/I, p. 330; *OC*, p. 379; *S*, p. 290). Lacking the "force of reason," he says they are "ᴬ like the animals, who have no knowledge of their young except while they cling to their dugs." And if lack of intellect is a fault in women, he seems to hold it even more against them that instinct itself does not bind them to love their offspring with constancy:

ᴬ Moreover, it is easy to see by experience that this natural affection, to which we give so much authority, has very weak roots. Every day we take their own children out of the arms of mothers, and make them take charge of ours, for a very slight profit. We make them abandon their own to some wretched nurse to whom we do not want to entrust our own, or to some goat; forbidding them not only to give them suck, whatever danger they may thereby incur, but even to take any care of them, that they may be entirely employed in the service of ours. And we see in most of them a bastard affection soon engendered by habit, more vehement than the natural, and a greater solicitude for the preservation of the borrowed children than for their own. . . . Animals alter and corrupt their natural affection as easily as we. (*DB*/I, pp. 330–31; *OC*, pp. 379–80; *S*, pp. 290–91.)

This long condemnation of motherly instinct (made even more bitter by the omitted passage, which concerns the custom of using goats to suckle children) assumes added force when we recall that Montaigne himself was taken from his mother to be nursed by a peasant woman in a nearby village until the age of two. This procedure, which he explains as a plan of his father's to bring him closer to the common people, was in fact a fairly general practice among the French nobility of his time. The early separation, followed by several years during which Montaigne's mother was allowed to speak to him only in Latin (which she scarcely knew), seems to have established a permanent distance between them. She may have openly disapproved of his upbringing, and it appears that she favored her younger children. It is not surprising that Montaigne scarcely mentions his mother throughout the essays. Both Michel and his father seem to have taken it for granted that women, though useful and necessary creatures and a delight to the senses, could not be *loved*—indeed, were not normally capable of a true communion of souls. And the spouses that both chose of course matched this opinion: excellent household managers and dutiful child-bearers, but probably little more.[1]

Between fathers and sons much more was possible—provided one had sons. The misfortune that Montaigne laments between the lines of this essay is that his wife has borne him five daughters (four of whom have died in infancy) and no sons.[2] Life and death seemed to conspire to deprive him of all opportunities for deep and lasting affection, at least on his terms. In such extremities, Montaigne's erotic project takes the form of a book. For this, too, we can thank his father, whose affection had been offered, above all, as a reward for literary accomplishments. (And perhaps the tutor who contrived to let him read Ovid on the sly should share some of the credit.) I do not mean to say simply that the essays were preordained by childhood influences. The point is that at a crucial stage in his life, when so many of his chances for intimacy had been frustrated, Montaigne summoned up his strongest resources: his talents for self-observation, identification, and verbal expression. And with these he achieved a remarkable integrity. His new direction of growth, in fact, was an evolutionary change in the structure of selfhood. As I have

[1] See "Of Friendship" (*OC*, p. 185; *S*, p. 138). Although in III: 3 (*OC*, pp. 804–5; *S*, p. 627) Montaigne expresses a preference for a mistress of some mental capacities, he makes it quite plain that bodily considerations come first, and affection never seems to enter the picture. My estimates here rely on Frame's thorough research and cautious conjectures in *Montaigne: A Biography*, Chapters II and VI.

[2] A sixth daughter, who also died, was born in 1583.

suggested in Chapter Six, he became whole by expanding himself to include his book.

That this essay is Montaigne's vehicle for transcending his erotic frustration is affirmed by a review of its content, for everything in it relates to the desire to make himself loved. The conspicuous dedication to a titled lady, for instance—a device that he employed in several essays during this period—betrays a concern for his reputation among his own class. He is at great pains to avoid being thought of as a professional writer, and to parade his social connections and the affection in which he is held by the nobility. His strategy is to disarm criticism with confessions of ineptitude, and his candor in doing so is primarily intended to charm. In this, the essay usually gets the desired response, even when its intention is obvious. Montaigne's choice of Mme d'Estissac in this instance is doubly significant: we can see how he must have envied her for having a son to receive her enlightened care, and how he must have envied the son who had such an accomplished and affectionate mother. Indeed, it was this same young man that he took with him two years later on his journey to Italy.

The body of the essay (the dedication appears to be an extraneous appendage[3]) begins by opposing instinct to reason, contrasting infants and animals to educated men. That Montaigne should approach his topic from this particular standpoint reflects, I think, the natural ambivalence he has felt in his relation to his father. A strong emotional attachment between the two obviously existed from Michel's earliest years; and this tie must have occasioned considerable guilt when Michel realized that he must both survive and displace his beloved parent.

To argue that this conflict is an inevitable consequence of

---

[3] This may explain why Montaigne, after dedicating the essay to an admirably accomplished mother, goes on to condemn women as ignoble and faithless creatures of instinct.

the life cycle is a "rational" consolation for the "instinctual" dilemma—a consolation of which Montaigne availed himself at least as early as 1572, in the essay entitled "One Man's Profit Is Another Man's Harm." By resuming the argument here, he reveals that his literary reflections on parental affection cover a strong undercurrent of emotion. They are a working out, at the level of ideas, of the dominant intention of his life: to attract and retain his father's love.

Thus the manifest function of the essay as a whole is directly related to Montaigne's most personal experience. He is concerned about the widespread failure of his class to provide for their sons, a failure that betokens either a lack of love or a foolish reluctance to express love. The folly, the danger, and the pathos of this vice are apparent to him because he has known both the warmth of paternal radiance and the chill of its disappearance.[4] His further concern with wills, dowries, and maternal domination is also based on personal experience. Frame's account of Michel's relations with his mother after Pierre's death deals largely with these matters of finance and control of the household; and there is a striking lack of evidence for affection between mother and son. It is on the issue of allowing mothers to interfere in their sons' inheritances that Montaigne unleashes his almost vicious attack on the faithlessness of women who do not nurse their own children.

---

[4] We might infer from the following passage in "Of Friendship" that his father, too, held him somewhat at a distance after the early years of special indulgence had come to an end: "ᴬ From children toward fathers, it is rather respect. Friendship feeds on communication, which cannot exist between them because of their too great inequality, and might perhaps interfere with the duties of nature. For neither can all the secret thoughts of fathers be communicated to children, lest this beget an unbecoming intimacy, nor could the admonitions and corrections, which are one of the chief duties of friendship, be administered by children to fathers. There have been nations where by custom the children killed their fathers, and others where the fathers killed their children, to avoid the interference that they can sometimes cause each other; and by nature the one depends on the destruction of the other" (*DB*/I, p. 137; *OC*, p. 183; *S*, p. 136).

We come now to a transition of the greatest importance, fully as revealing as the one that moves from "me faire aymer" to the story of Monluc. Montaigne has just concluded his tirade on mothers who "bastardize" natural affection. The next paragraph begins thus:

^ Now when we consider this simple reason for loving our children—that we begot them, wherefore we call them flesh of our flesh and bone of our bone—it seems to me that there is indeed another production proceeding from us that is no less commendable. For what we engender by the soul, the children of our mind and our ability, are produced by a nobler part than the body and are more our own. We are father and mother both in this generation. These cost us a lot more, and bring us more honor, if they have any good in them. (*DB*/I, pp. 331–32; *OC*, pp. 380–81; *S*, p. 291.)

Almost immediately thereafter Montaigne abandons the relatively mature style in which the essay has been written so far and reverts to his custom of six years before, collecting and commenting on a series of examples from history to illustrate his point. We can almost see him reliving, in crude outline, the gradual process by which he has given up hope of deriving emotional satisfaction from his family relationships and fled for comfort to his books on ancient history. He cites first the case of Labienus, whose books were burnt by the Roman state:

^ It was with him that this new sort of penalty began, which was later continued in Rome against many others, of punishing by death even writings and studies. There was not enough means and matter for cruelty unless we brought in things which nature has exempted from all feeling and all suffering, such as reputation and the inventions of our mind, and unless we communicated corporal punishments to the teachings and monuments of the muses. (*DB*/I, p. 333; *OC*, p. 381; *S*, p. 292.)

One of the things this example says is that books and achievements are exempt from feeling, from suffering, and normally from death. Thus, because they are immortal, the doctrines of an Epicurus, the writings of an Augustine, and the victories of an Epaminondas, Alexander, or Caesar are to be valued above any children the men may have had. It is obvious that to Montaigne his book is a father and a friend that can never die, and that it takes the place of a son who was never born.

But this substitution is not without problems, one of which is that books, being exempted by nature from feeling and mortality, are "unnatural" objects for our love. Hence the essay ends with a vision of the statue of Galatea, quickening from ivory into flesh under the incestuous caress of its creator.

I said earlier that this essay "drifts off" into the realm of imagination, never to return to its concrete concerns. It is thus symbolic of the process by which Montaigne transcends his emotional and social frustrations through imagination. The dialectic we have observed in other essays, by which anxiety and imagination, body and mind, conformity and rebellion, modesty and self-assertion, player and role were all integrated in a self at once whole and complex, is visible here as well. But the ambiguous image of Pygmalion at the end reminds us of the dangers and limitations of transcendence through art. In this essay, at least, imagination looks disturbingly like an escape from involvement with flesh-and-blood men.

The turn from physical to imaginative procreation is greatly accentuated in successive versions of the essay. Early in the 1588 text, Montaigne expands on the topic of his early upbringing. He was never subjected to force, he says, and has likewise eschewed force in the discipline of his own children, although "ᴮ they all die on me at nurse" (*OC*, p. 369; *S*, p. 281). The flippancy of this phrase has shocked some critics who failed to see in it a defense against suffering. It probably also reflects Montaigne's deep resentment that all his offspring were female. Two sentences later, still on the subject of gentle

treatment, he declares: "ᴮ I should have been much more scrupulous still in this respect toward boys."

Further on, he sharpens his attack on women, who are "always inclined to cross their husbands" (*OC*, p. 374; *S*, p. 286).
And although he makes an effort to be as open as possible with
his family, in order to avoid misunderstanding (*OC*, p. 376;
S, p. 288), there is no suggestion that he enjoys their intimacy.
His final addition to the text of this date frankly admits the
temptation to reject flesh for fancy: "ᴮ And I do not know
whether I would not like much better to have produced one
perfectly formed child by intercourse with the muses than by
intercourse with my wife" (*OC*, p. 383; *S*, p. 293).

The changes made after 1588 are more expansive and even
more explicit. It now seems quite natural and fitting to Montaigne that he should love his book. Did not Aristotle say that
of all workmen the poet is most especially enamored of his
work? (*Ibid.*) And Montaigne's book, as he boasts in the
opening paragraph, is the only one of its kind (*OC*, p. 364;
S, p. 278). Embroidering further on Aristotle, he reasons that
every man exists within his work in some sense by virtue of
the activity he expends on it, for "being consists in movement
and action" (*OC*, p. 366; *S*, p. 279).

Plato's theory of erotic sublimation provides Montaigne
with more fruitful models. He quotes, from the dialogues,
opinions on the desirability of marrying late and of abstain-
ing from sex in the pursuit of higher goals (*OC*, pp. 369–70;
S, p. 282). And he cites Plato's opinion that great works are
immortal children that can in turn immortalize or even deify
their fathers (*OC*, p. 381; *S*, p. 291).

Extending his account of an elderly miser who was constantly deceived by his family, to whom he gave neither love
nor money, Montaigne goes so far as to call wife, son, and
servant "ᵒ so many enemies to us" (*OC*, p. 375; *S*, p. 286). Far
from exempting his own family from this charge, he says he

is quite as deceivable (*pipable*) as the next man; but unlike the miser, who tries to defend himself against fraud, Montaigne simply diverts his attention from it. In simpler terms, he turns his back on those around him and retires to amuse himself with his book.

Thus far I have attempted to show how an understanding of Montaigne's erotic predicament illuminates the structure and development of his essay. I should like to conclude by selecting two late additions that epitomize this predicament.

In the very midst of his laments about the lack of love in marriage, Montaigne suddenly reverts to thoughts of friendship: "ᶜ And will it ever be said enough how precious is a friend, and how different a thing from these civil bonds?" (*OC*, p. 375; *S*, pp. 286–87). In his own copy of the *Essays*, he went even further, penning into the margin the following meditation on his feeling for La Boétie:

> ᶜ Am I better off for having had the taste of it, or am I worse off? Certainly I am better off. My regret for him consoles and honors me. Is it not a pious and pleasant duty of my life to be forever performing his obsequies? Is there an enjoyment that is worth this privation?[5]

Near the end of his life, he still mourns his lost love. And what he might ordinarily have bestowed on a son, he gives to his book:

> ᶜ To this child, such as it is, what I give I give purely and irrevocably, as one gives to the children of one's body. The little good I have done for it is no longer at my disposal. It may know a good

---

[5] *OC*, p. 376n; *S*, p. 286n. The passage does not appear in the body of either text because, as Frame's note explains, it was revised, moved, and eventually crossed out by Montaigne (or possibly by someone else). Although it appears (at a different location) in the 1595 edition, modern editors are not quite sure what to do with it. For our purposes, it is important to note that its *authenticity* is not in doubt, even though its treatment in the text is problematic.

many things that I no longer know and hold from me what I have not retained and what, just like a stranger, I should have to borrow from it if I came to need it. If I am wiser than it, it is richer than I. (*OC*, p. 383; *S*, p. 293.)

In the juxtaposition of these attitudes, I think, we can grasp something essential about Montaigne, at least as he appears in his book. He longs continually for affection and continually seeks to win it by being seductive, that is, by putting himself on exhibition and making himself lovable. At the same time, he continually transforms his experience into images, ideas, and eventually essays. Each such transformation wrests a moment of his experience from the mortality that has repeatedly overtaken his love. But it also "fixes" the experience, as Galatea was fixed in ivory. A work of art may reflect the warmth we put into it, but it never generates any of its own; the wish to bring it to life is idle. The myth of Pygmalion is an instance of magical thinking, and magic is ultimately impotent against death.

In Chapter Six we saw that by constructing his self-image Montaigne gained power over himself. In the present chapter we see that he had another aim as well: to invite intimate contact with other human beings. Self-knowledge is essential to the former task, but intimacy presents a problem that the most transparent self-understanding cannot solve. True, he succeeds in disclosing to his readers a wealth of personal detail, some of it deeply felt. But two other factors must qualify the success of the essays as an erotic project. The first, which we have just been observing, is narcissism: Montaigne becomes enamored not of his reader but of his book. The second is the necessary impersonality of contacts between author and public: his deepest revelations are made to persons most of whom he will never see. This paradox of the literary medium will be the topic of my concluding chapter.

9. Medium and Mediacy

Thus far I have discussed essays ranging from Montaigne's earliest and most impersonal efforts to the frankly self-revelatory achievements with which he completed his first two books. Their sequence tells one kind of a story: how, over the years, his own character and opinions gradually replaced abstract questions as the subject of his writing; how he gave increased attention to social issues such as education, government, and parenthood (and others I have not discussed, such as medicine and primitive peoples); and how, the more he focused on his own experience of these things, the more he found to say and the more boldly he said it.

I have also analyzed the differences between the three versions of each separate essay. This analysis tells us much more. First, it reveals the problems Montaigne was trying to solve in the early stages of his writing: the anxiety attendant on imaginative freedom; the fear of bodily decay; the conflict between liberal opinions and political security; the bad faith involved in professions of modesty; the artifice required for effective role-playing; and finally, a frustrated need for admiration and affection. Second, and most important, the comparison reveals how his style evolved as a solution to these problems. His increasing playfulness, evasiveness, and even trickery are a response to brute facts of human existence such as death, disease, and impotence, which cannot be resisted head-on. A feminine sort of receptivity relieves his earlier guardedness. He cultivates nonchalance, unruliness, and apparent disorder because of their resemblance to bodily spontaneity. Moods of rebellion and reaction, obstinacy and irony, give way to one another in organic rhythm.

Montaigne's new relaxation and flexibility allow for change and growth. At the same time, his emerging self-image provides him with identity. Reflecting on his habits and opinions, he distinguishes what is authentic from what is borrowed; later, reflecting on his writing, he recognizes his own duplicity and transcends it by divulging it. One after another, he masters his conflicts by setting them at a distance and then synthesizing their opposing claims. The published essays are the frame in which his contradictions can be contained.

But there is an opposing trend that also emerges in the successive versions of the text. Starting from his identification with La Boétie—so close a bond that he calls it both "union" and "confusion"—he attains distance from himself only by increasing the distance between himself and others. Thus his pursuit of intimacy takes the paradoxical form of more frequent withdrawal from the world.

All these observations help us to unfold the structure of individual essays and reveal the psychological function of their changes in form. But the structure of the essays is also the structure of the man, and our literary analysis has also been a psychoanalysis. Let me conclude this study with an explanation of what I think that means. It will be helpful to refer, in this connection, not to any of the essays published in 1580 and twice revised, but to one of the essays in the third book, where Montaigne's self-awareness is mature from the beginning and his distinctive style of self-presentation fully elaborated. I shall therefore illustrate some of my points with passages from III: 3, "Of Three Kinds of Association," although my remarks are not intended as an interpretation of that entire essay.

The Self, as I have conceived of it in these pages, is an ideal entity constructed by the ego as an intermediary between the ego and others. It is the source of one's identity, but it originates, paradoxically, in that moment when a child identifies with the Other. He grasps the unity of his self-perceptions— that is, the Self to which they refer—by putting himself in the place of another subject. He stands, in imagination, "outside himself" in order to look back in.

The distance between the ego and the Self, and the difference between them, are obscured by language, which teaches us that "I" and "me" are the same entity existing in the alternate modes of subject and object. This confusion is natural, since language is the medium of our intersubjectivity. We can communicate with other men because we have adopted their language, the voice of their inwardness, as the expression of our own; and we identify in some way with the Other each time we use his words. The Self is an object for the ego just as it is an object for the Other because the ego has had to adopt the language of the Other in order to *have* a Self. Without language, I would not know who I am, and you would not know what I am—to wit, a man like yourself.

As the Self mediates between ego and Other, so it mediates between Becoming and Being. It consists, for the most part, of memories of everything one has done, felt, and been. It has arrested the evanescence and diversity of countless self-perceptions in order to comprehend and possess them. Though it refers to the past, it has a future, for its existence is perpetuated by each new and unpredictable movement of the ego. The "I" that creates the "me" is a free agent, continuously involved in the process of Becoming, and its choices in the present moment become in the next instant the permanent content of the Self.

No one was more keenly aware than Montaigne of both the need for identity and the need for freedom:

^B It is existing, but not living, to keep ourselves bound and obliged by necessity to a single course. The fairest souls are those that have the most variety and adaptability. If it were up to me to train myself in my own fashion, there is no way so good that I should want to be fixed in it and unable to break loose. Life is an uneven, irregular, and multiform movement. We are not friends to ourselves, and still less masters, we are slaves, if we follow ourselves incessantly and are so caught in our inclinations that we cannot depart from them or twist them about. (*OC*, p. 796; *S*, p. 621.)

The motive for identity formation is self-mastery. In order to function in the social world one must be "maistre de soy," and self-study reassures Montaigne that there is indeed "une forme maistresse," a ruling pattern in the bewildering multiplicity of his attitudes. But how easily one can become enslaved by attachment to a chosen style of existence! He sees that even introspection can be addictive if carried to excess. If one is to be master rather than slave of one's Self, one must leave an opening for movement, change, and spontaneity. If one is to live and not simply to be, one must continually revise and reform the Self.

Since language is the chief vehicle of our selfhood and since Montaigne's book is an effort to put his Self into words, these words must be both lively and perdurable. His style, therefore, is designed to vibrate between Becoming and Being. On the one hand, he "paints his portrait," fixing his image in the highly abstract and indefinitely reproduceable medium of print. On the other hand, he "talks to his book," to such good effect that centuries later his writing can create the illusion that he is a personal acquaintance whose presence is an event in our lives. In the following passage (from III: 3), notice how particular self-observations alternate with generalizations, and how sententious philosophy alternates with homely metaphor and seemingly spontaneous exclamations:

^B Now to go on with my subject, this fastidious disposition makes me hard to please in dealings with men—I have to cull them out on the sorting tray—and makes me ill-fitted for ordinary actions. We live and deal with plain people. If association with them is a burden to us, if we disdain to adjust ourselves to humble and vulgar souls—and the humble and vulgar ones are often as well-regulated as the subtler ones ^C (all wisdom is foolish that does not adapt itself to the common folly —^B we should no longer meddle with either our own affairs or those of others: both private and public affairs are worked out with these people. The least strained and most natural ways of the soul are the most beautiful; the best occupations are the least forced. Lord, what a favor wisdom does for those whose desires she adjusts to their power! There is no more useful knowledge. "According to one's power," that was the refrain and favorite saying of Socrates, a saying of great substance. We must direct and fix our desires on the easiest and nearest things. Is it not a stupid humor of mine to be out of tune with a thousand to whom I am joined by fortune, whom I cannot do without, only to cling to one or two, who are not associated with me, or rather to a fantastic desire for something I cannot recapture? My easygoing ways, opposed to all bitterness and asperity, may very well have relieved me of envy and hostility; to be loved I will not say, but no man ever gave more occasion not to be hated. But the coolness of my dealings has rightly robbed me of the good will of many, who are to be excused for interpreting it in another and worse sense. (*OC*, pp. 797–98; *S*, p. 622.)

Flexibility is the essence of Montaigne's language, as it is of his philosophy. He has abandoned Latin, a language completely controlled by writing, for a vernacular that is changing so fast, he says, that it escapes every day from his hands. And then, since any language tends to act as a closed system, he stretches the boundaries of literary French with personal and regional eccentricities, syntactical shortcuts, and conversational rhythms.[1] Protesting that his thoughts cannot be expressed in deeds, he struggles to embody them instead in "this airy medium of words" (*ce corps aerée de la voix*).

The essay "Of Three Kinds of Association" also reminds us that Montaigne's literary project was designed to bridge a widening gap between himself and others. It describes the three occupations he likes best: conversation with "honnestes et habiles hommes" who are capable of true friendship; flirtation with attractive women, in whom intelligence is a recommendation second to beauty; and a relaxed familiarity with books, "the best provision I have found for this human journey." In his youthful affairs with women he had "burnt himself" occasionally, and had eventually learned to be neither too hot nor too detached. Age has in any case diminished his opportunities for that kind of sport. To gentlemen of talent he is an ardent friend:

ᴮ I am very capable of forming and maintaining rare and exquisite friendships, inasmuch as I grasp so hungrily at any acquaintances that suit my taste, I make advances and I throw myself at them so avidly, that I hardly fail to attach myself and to make an impression wherever I land. I have often made happy proof of this. In ordinary friendships I am somewhat barren and cool, for my pace is not natural if it is not under full sail. Besides, my fortune, having trained me from my youth for a single perfect friendship and given me a taste for it, has in truth given me a certain distaste for the others; and has imprinted too deeply on my fancy that friendship is an animal made for company, not for the herd, as that ancient said. And furthermore, by nature I find it hard to

---

[1] These features of Montaigne's style have been so thoroughly discussed elsewhere that I shall spare the reader further examples. Compare Auerbach, "L'Humaine Condition"; Buffum, *Studies in the Baroque*. On the relation of speech and hearing to Becoming and of print and sight to Being, see Ong, *The Presence of the Word*; McLuhan, *The Gutenberg Galaxy*; and Jonas, *The Phenomenon of Life*, pp. 135–56. For an analysis of Montaigne's need to fix his being, see Poulet, "Montaigne," in *Studies in Human Time*.

communicate myself by halves and moderately. (*OC*, p. 798; *S*, p. 623.)

On closer inspection, it appears that Montaigne's "rare and exquisite friendships" have been few and shortlived, and his reckless advances disproportionate to the return:

[B] Is it not a stupid humor of mine to be out of tune with a thousand to whom I am joined by fortune, whom I cannot do without, only to cling to one or two, who are not associated with me, or rather to a fantastic desire for something I cannot recapture? (*OC*, p. 798; *S*, p. 622.)

The death of La Boétie has taught Montaigne the danger of giving oneself unreservedly to another person. Books are less perishable:

[B] These two kinds of association [conversation and love] are accidental and dependent on others. One is annoying by its rarity, the other withers with age; thus they would not have provided well enough for the needs of my life. Association with books, which is the third kind, is much more certain and more our own. (*OC*, p. 805; *S*, p. 628.)

His tendency to spend ever more time with his books finds expression in the final pages of the essay, where in version *C* he expands the description of the tower library from which, in jealously guarded privacy, he looks down on the life of his estate (*OC*, pp. 806–7; *S*, p. 629).

We see here a gradual withdrawal from direct personal confrontation to a less risky position. The movement has public as well as private dimensions: from the polemical atmosphere of the Parlement (where he was noted for his "customary vivacity," not to say temper) and the court (where he was thought to be "meddlesome") Montaigne withdrew to criticize society in writing. But neither in public nor in private did his withdrawal signify repudiation or isolation, because in each case the essays reestablished contact. For the "hot" medium of voice and gesture, he substituted the "cooler" medium of print. He, who found it hard to communicate himself moderately or by halves, came to the realization "that in using our minds, we have more need, for the most part, of lead than of wings, of coolness and repose than of ardor and agitation" (*OC*, p. 799; *S*, p. 624).

That Montaigne has found his own best medium—indeed, has invented a medium for himself—is due to his irrepressible sociability. However paradoxical it may seem, he is right when he declares:

> B There are private, retiring, and inward natures. My essential pattern is suited to communication and revelation. I am all in the open and in full view, born for company and friendship. The solitude that I love and preach is primarily nothing but leading my feelings and thoughts back to myself, restraining and shortening not my steps, but my desires and my cares, abandoning solicitude for outside things, and mortally avoiding servitude and obligation, ° and not so much the press of people as the press of business. B Solitude of place, to tell the truth, rather makes me stretch and expand outward; I throw myself into affairs of state and into the world more readily when I am alone. (*OC*, p. 801; *S*, p. 625.)

One cannot be "all in the open and in full view" when one is pressed up against other people. Thorough self-revelation requires both the protection and the perspective provided by distance. Across the distance created by Montaigne's withdrawal, the *Essays* communicate him to us. In style as much as in content, they reach for both intimacy and persuasive power.

To the extent that public influence is more of a one-way relation than personal friendship, the *Essays* no doubt succeeded better in their bid for power than in their attempt at intimacy. Montaigne could talk endlessly to his book, but it could give him no more than an echo in reply. By substituting a visual for a vocal medium, he escaped important restraints and enlarged his audience incalculably; but he had to admit that conversation ultimately was more precious to him than sight (*OC*, p. 900; *S*, p. 704). Even on his deathbed, he is said to have wished for someone with whom he could converse.

As the form in which he managed to put himself in evidence, and as the chief vehicle of his commerce with other men, the *Essays* embody a large portion of Montaigne's existence. Their movement truly reflects the movement of life itself—in this case an intensely self-conscious life in which the highly charged distances between self and Other and between ego and Self must be constantly preserved and articulated, measured and spanned. For it is not only the function of the Self as a social go-between that is revealed (and to some extent performed) by this book. Montaigne's greatest achievement is to have caught in his mirror the inner oscillation between object and subject, between being and process, between identity and freedom. His self-image is an image not of the static Self but of the constant interplay that is the essence of self-consciousness. The distance between Montaigne and his book is used to reflect the distance between the invisible ego and its Self. His truth is the mediacy of selfhood.

Bibliography

Bibliography

d'Aubigné, Théodore Agrippa. "Sa vie à ses enfants," in *Oeuvres complètes*, I, 1–113. Paris: Alphonse Lemerre, 1873.

Auerbach, Erich. "L'Humaine Condition," pp. 249–73 in *Mimesis*, translated by Willard Trask. Garden City, N.Y.: Doubleday Anchor, 1957.

Berger, Harry, Jr., and H. M. Leicester, Jr. *An Approach to a Working Model of Period Consciousness: Toward Interpretation*. Unpublished paper, University of California at Santa Cruz, 1969.

Berger, Peter L., and Thomas Luckmann. *The Social Construction of Reality: A Treatise in the Sociology of Knowledge*. Garden City, N.Y.: Doubleday Anchor, 1967.

Bitton, Davis. *The French Nobility in Crisis: 1560–1640*. Stanford, Calif.: Stanford University Press, 1969.

Brown, Norman O. *Love's Body*. New York: Random House, 1966.

Buffum, Imbrie. *Studies in the Baroque from Montaigne to Rotrou*. New Haven: Yale University Press, 1957.

Castiglione, Baldesar. *The Book of the Courtier*, translated by Charles S. Singleton. Garden City, N.Y.: Doubleday Anchor, 1959.

Curtius, Ernst Robert. *European Literature and the Latin Middle Ages*, translated by Willard R. Trask. New York: Pantheon, 1953.

Douce, Francis, and Thomas Frognall Dibdin. *The Dance of Death and Holbein's Bible Cuts*. London, 1896.

Erikson, Erik H. *Childhood and Society*, 2d ed. New York: Norton, 1963.

Bibliography

—— *Identity: Youth and Crisis.* New York: Norton, 1968.

—— *Insight and Responsibility: Lectures on the Ethical Implications of Psychoanalytic Insight.* New York: Norton, 1964.

—— *Young Man Luther: A Study in Psychoanalysis and History.* New York: Norton, 1962. (Original publ. 1958.)

Febvre, Lucien. *Le Problème de l'incroyance au XVIe siècle: la religion de Rabelais.* Paris: A. Michel, 1947.

Frame, Donald M. *Montaigne: A Biography.* New York: Harcourt, Brace & World, 1965.

—— *Montaigne's Discovery of Man: The Humanization of a Humanist.* New York: Columbia University Press, 1955.

Goffman, Erving. *The Presentation of Self in Everyday Life.* Garden City, N.Y.: Doubleday Anchor, 1959.

—— "Role Distance," pp. 83–152 in *Encounters: Two Studies in the Sociology of Interaction.* New York: Bobbs-Merrill, 1961.

Goldstein, Kurt. *Human Nature in the Light of Psychopathology.* New York: Schocken, 1963. (Original publ. 1940.)

Hall, Calvin S., and Gardner Lindzey. *Theories of Personality,* 2d ed. New York: Wiley, 1970.

Heidegger, Martin. *Being and Time,* translated by John Macquarrie and Edward Robinson. New York: Harper & Row, 1962.

Jansen, Frederik J. B. *Sources vives de la pensée de Montaigne: Étude sur les fondements psychologiques et biographiques des Essais.* Copenhagen: Levin and Munksgaard, 1935.

Jonas, Hans. *The Phenomenon of Life: Toward a Philosophical Biology.* New York: Dell, 1968.

Kierkegaard, Soren. *The Concept of Dread,* translated by Walter Lowrie. 2d ed. Princeton, N.J.: Princeton University Press, 1957.

Lacan, Jacques. "Le stade du miroir comme formateur de la fonction du Je," pp. 93–100 in *Ecrits.* Paris: Editions du Seuil, 1966.

—— "The Function of Language in Psychoanalysis," in *The Language of the Self,* translated with notes and commentary by Anthony Wilden. Baltimore: Johns Hopkins Press, 1968.

Lapp, John C. *The Esthetics of Negligence: La Fontaine's Contes.* Cambridge, Eng.: Cambridge University Press, 1971.

McLuhan, Marshall. *The Gutenberg Galaxy.* Toronto: University of Toronto Press, 1965. (Original publ. 1962.)

Mâle, Emile. *L'Art religieux de la fin du Moyen Age en France,* 5th ed. Paris: Armand Colin, 1949.

Mead, George H. *Mind, Self, and Society from the Standpoint of a Social Behaviorist.* Chicago: University of Chicago Press, 1934.

Bibliography

Merleau-Ponty, Maurice. *The Structure of Behavior*, translated by Alden L. Fisher. Boston: Beacon, 1963.

Montaigne, Michel de. *The Complete Essays of Montaigne* [*S*], translated by Donald M. Frame. Stanford, Calif.: Stanford University Press, 1958.

——— *Essais de Michel de Montaigne: Texte original de 1580 avec les variantes des éditions de 1582 et 1587* [*DB*], R. Dezeimeris and H. Barckhausen, eds. 2 vols. Bordeaux: Féret, 1870–73. This is the only modern edition that allows the reader to see at a glance the form in which these essays were originally published.

——— *Oeuvres complètes de Montaigne* [*OC*], Albert Thibaudet and Maurice Rat, eds. Paris: Gallimard, 1962.

Ong, Walter J., S.J. *The Presence of the Word: Some Prolegomena for Cultural and Religious History*. New Haven: Yale University Press, 1967.

Poulet, Georges. *Studies in Human Time*, translated by Elliott Coleman. Baltimore: Johns Hopkins Press, 1956.

Santayana, George. *Soliloquies in England and Later Soliloquies*. New York: Scribner's, 1922.

Sartre, Jean-Paul. *The Psychology of Imagination*, translated by Bernard Frechtman. New York: Washington Square, 1966.

——— *The Transcendence of the Ego: An Existentialist Theory of Consciousness*, translated by Forrest Williams and Robert Kirkpatrick. New York: Noonday, 1957.

Seneca, Lucius Annaeus. *Ad Lucilium Epistulae Morales*, with English translation by Richard M. Gummere. 3 vols. Cambridge, Mass.: Harvard University Press, 1917–25. Vol. III rev. 1953.

Strowski, Fortunat. *Montaigne: Sa vie publique et privée*. Paris: Nouvelle Revue Critique, 1938.

Tillich, Paul. *The Courage to Be*. New Haven: Yale University Press, 1952.

Trinquet, Roger. *La Jeunesse de Montaigne: Ses origines familiales, son enfance et ses études*. Paris: Nizet, 1972.

Villey, Pierre. *Les Sources et l'évolution des Essais de Montaigne*, 2d ed. 2 vols. Paris: Hachette, 1933.

Wilden, Anthony. *"Par divers moyens on arrive à pareille fin*: A Reading of Montaigne," *Modern Language Notes*, 83 (1968), 577–97.

Index

Index

Index

Index